Jesus 101

Radical Discipleship

ORDINARY PEOPLE ACCEPTING EXTRA-ORDINARY Grace

Aivars Ozolins, PhD
with
Elizabeth Viera Talbot, PhD

Pacific Press®
Publishing Association
Nampa, Idaho | Oshawa, Ontario, Canada
www.pacificpress.com

Cover image from iStockphoto.com
Inside design by Aaron Troia
Jesus 101 logo designed by Steve Trapero

Copyright © 2016 by Pacific Press® Publishing Association
Printed in the United States of America
All rights reserved

The authors assume full responsibility for the accuracy of all facts and quotations as cited in this book.

Unless otherwise indicated, Scripture quotations are from the NEW AMERICAN STANDARD BIBLE®, Copyright © 1960, 1962, 1963, 1968, 1971, 1972, 1973, 1975, 1977, 1995 by The Lockman Foundation. Used by permission.

Scripture quotations marked NIV are from THE HOLY BIBLE, NEW INTERNATIONAL VERSION®, NIV®. Copyright © 1973, 1978, 1984, 2011 by Biblica, Inc.® Used by permission. All rights reserved worldwide.

Scripture quotations marked NLT are taken from the Holy Bible, New Living Translation, copyright © 1996, 2004, 2007, 2013, 2015 by Tyndale House Foundation. Used by permission of Tyndale House Publishers, Inc., Carol Stream, Illinois 60188. All rights reserved.

Scriptures quoted from RSV are from the Revised Standard Version of the Bible, copyright © 1946, 1952, and 1971 by the Division of Christian Education of the National Council of the Churches of Christ in the United States of America. Used by permission. All rights reserved.

You can obtain additional copies of this book by calling toll-free 1-800-765-6955 or by visiting http://www.adventistbookcenter.com.

Library of Congress Cataloging-in-Publication Data

Names: Ozolins, Aivars, author.
Title: Radical discipleship / Aivars Ozolins, with Elizabeth Viera Talbot.
Description: Nampa : Pacific Press Publishing, 2016.
Identifiers: LCCN 2016004074 | ISBN 978-0-8163-6160-1 (pbk.)
Subjects: LCSH: Christian life. | Discipling (Christianity) | Jesus
 Christ—Calling of the twelve.
Classification: LCC BV4501.3 .O97 2016 | DDC 248.4—dc23 LC record available at http://lccn.loc.gov/2016004074

April 2016

Dedication

We dedicate this book to all those
who have been bruised and battered
in trying hard to keep it all together;
to those who have attempted to do right,
but know the taste of failure and defeat;
to those disciples who have sensed
the call of Jesus, "Follow Me," but
have realized their powerlessness.
We pray that this book will give
you hope as you gaze into the
beautiful face of Jesus and
realize the amazing truth
of His grace. We are
broken vessels of clay,
flawed and wounded; yet in the
Potter's capable hands we have been
entrusted with the treasure of the gospel!

And to Jesus, our Master,
whose extraordinary *grace*
makes it *all possible* and *worthwhile*!

Table of Contents

Introduction 7

EXTRA-Ordinary Choice 9

EXTRA-Ordinary Forgiveness 13

EXTRA-Ordinary Love 17

EXTRA-Ordinary Revelation 21

EXTRA-Ordinary Master 26

EXTRA-Ordinary Insight 31

EXTRA-Ordinary Acceptance 36

EXTRA-Ordinary Calling 41

EXTRA-Ordinary Compassion 45

EXTRA-Ordinary Worth 49

EXTRA-Ordinary Perseverance 54

EXTRA-Ordinary Encounter 59

Introduction

Dear Reader and Friend:

I am so excited to start another journey through the Bible together with you. I can't wait to see what insights you will gain and how the Holy Spirit will motivate you in new ways to follow Jesus without any reservations! He is the Author and Finisher of our faith! He is the A and the Z!

This book was conceived when one of our scholars in residence, Aivars Ozolins, PhD, who is a member of the Jesus 101 executive committee and the outside editor for all of our books, did some research on the disciples of Jesus, for a *Jesus 101* TV series that Mike Tucker, MEd, (speaker/director for www.faithfortoday.tv) and I were about to tape. I really enjoyed Aivars's research, and a very successful TV series was born: *Radical Discipleship.* This series, which is still airing on several channels, seemed to answer questions for many people who were wondering: who can be a disciple of Jesus and who *really* qualifies? The TV series *Radical Discipleship,* with twelve programs, is now available on three DVDs as a companion to this book. The set is designed for group or personal study, matching each video presentation with a chapter in the book, including study questions at the end of each chapter. I highly recommend it for a deeper study of the subject. I asked Aivars if he would be willing to embark on a writing project with me based on his research, and he gladly accepted. That's how this booklet made it to your hands. That's why, even though we both contributed to this book, you will find stories from the other side of the world, not just from Argentina as in my previous books. Aivars is from Latvia, by the Baltic Sea, and many of the chapters start with very interesting stories from his early life there. I trust that you will find much relevant information and many insights in this book that will help you understand how Jesus treated his disciples and the extraordinary grace that He offers to us.

The main reason why I decided to add this book to the resources

Radical Discipleship

available through the Jesus 101 Biblical Institute is that I noticed that there are some misconceptions about discipleship. Some believe that the disciples of Jesus never make mistakes, never have bad moods, nor have difficult days. But that is totally nonbiblical! I have heard discipleship seminars that talk about endless victory and never-ending mountaintop experiences. And most of us cannot relate to that! Not even the biblical characters, other than Jesus, can relate to a life without sin, which none of us will ever have on this side of eternity! (See 1 John 1:8.) As a matter of fact, the twelve disciples of Jesus had many character flaws and were unlikely candidates to start a brand-new church! I personally would not have chosen them, but then again, I wouldn't choose myself either. So when we start studying each one of the disciples of Jesus, we find hope and purpose as well as forgiveness and compassion. We discover that they were ordinary people who found EXTRA-ordinary grace through Jesus Christ, their new Master. As they surrendered to that grace, they were in awe of how God used broken and wounded vessels for His glory and in order to advance His kingdom here on earth.

Discipleship is a reversal of values in light of the Cross. Radical discipleship is what happens when ordinary people accept EXTRA-ordinary grace, which overflows in ways that surprise everyone, including the disciples themselves! May you find that the grace of Jesus Christ is the greatest motivation for a life of purpose in Him. As imperfect as we are, the assurance of salvation is ours because of the merits of Jesus Christ, our Master! His perfect life and death are credited to us! That's why we are saved *only* by faith in Jesus! And that deserves a big Woo-hoo!!

Many heart-felt thanks to Pastor Mike Tucker, Dr. Aivars Ozolins, and to all who have contributed to this project. May all of us give our hearts to the Savior, and may all the glory and honor be for Jesus, who is the *only* Worthy One!

Many blessings,
Elizabeth Talbot, PhD
www.Jesus101.tv

Chapter 1

EXTRA-Ordinary Choice

Every day of our life is filled with choices, some are very important, others are less so. The impact of the choices we make varies widely. Some are almost inconsequential, such as deciding what to have for breakfast or what to wear for a dinner reception, others have monumental consequences that affect us for the rest of our lives, such as choosing one's career path or picking a spouse. Speaking of choosing a spouse, I remember how difficult and scary the decision was for me and my wife (of almost thirty-two happy years now). It was difficult, not because we did not love each other, or because we doubted whether we were a good match. It was the gravity of the decision that overwhelmed us. The day after we got engaged both of us got a serious case of cold feet. Back in our respective parents' homes we each agonized over it—what have we done? Is this really the right choice? Choices can be very difficult and heart-wrenching. And Jesus was about to make a choice of eternal significance . . .

I CHOOSE YOU!

When Jesus started His ministry, He had to make some extremely monumental choices too. He had to choose a team of His representatives who would follow Him and, after His ascension, continue His work. This team of people would be commissioned to form the nucleus of the early church and prepare it to carry the good news of salvation to the whole world. In view of this colossal task, we would expect Jesus to be very careful, selecting only the very best, highly qualified, and extraordinary people.

However, astonishingly, Jesus chose the most ordinary and flawed people. The people He selected were broken and dubious men with serious character flaws who would be disqualified for important jobs in our world. They were simple people from various walks of life and different trades and experiences; most likely without any, or very little, formal education. A few were fishermen; one was a Roman tax collector—a broadly hated and resented occupation. Another one came from a

Radical Discipleship

banished rebel movement, always ready to pick a fight with the establishment; still another one was a financier who was so enthralled with money and profit that he ended up selling his Master to the enemy. You look at them, and can't help exclaiming, "What in the world was Jesus thinking about when He chose them, this hodgepodge of misfits?" Yet, this band of ragtag apprentices chosen by Jesus spent three and a half years inspired and guided by Him, and in the end was transformed into a people of God who formed the core of His early church. God was able to use these constantly struggling, doubting, and failing, ordinary people to produce the most extraordinary results.

Significantly, the number of the disciples reminds us of the twelve similarly flawed and imperfect sons of Israel, whom God used to form His chosen people in the Old Testament. Now Jesus had selected twelve equally defective and broken disciples to form His church, and He made a point of reminding them that He had chosen them, "You didn't choose me. I chose you" (John 15:16, NLT). But *who* were these chosen ones?

SO, WHO QUALIFIES?

It is helpful to note the specific social honor pattern that permeated most every ancient culture. The honor system of the first century society formed a multilayer hierarchy in which each member of the society occupied a certain spot on the socioreligious ladder. The system strictly regulated relationships between individuals in social gatherings. Luke 14:8–10, where Jesus instructs His listeners not to take the highest place of honor in a banquet, is clearly indicative of this prevalent system. The same social structure naturally existed among the disciples. The hierarchy among them can be observed in the lists of the synoptic Gospels (Matthew 10:2–4; Mark 3:16–19; and Luke 6:14–16) as well as in the book of Acts (1:13), where they are presented in a consistent order, actually forming three distinct levels or circles of hierarchy.

Jesus, however, totally reversed the conventional values of social hierarchy and status. He turned the conventional norms upside down by introducing the kingdom principle of grace. Jesus taught that in order to be first we ought to be last, and if we are esteemed leaders in the eyes of God, it would be because we serve others. He had to teach the disciples a core lesson of equality in the kingdom: no one deserved it, and yet all were invited by grace. It was crucial for the disciples to understand that without Jesus they amounted to absolutely nothing, even when putting forward their very best efforts. But how can ordinary people become aware of such an extraordinary grace?

FROM ORDINARY TO EXTRA-ORDINARY

Luke and John team together to form an *inclusio* to make that very point, and it has to do with fishing. *Inclusio* is a "literary sandwich," where a narrative begins and ends with the same element. Early on in his Gospel, Luke recounts the calling of the first disciples. Peter had been fishing all night with absolutely no results. They are now washing the nets, which means they are done for the night. Jesus unexpectedly instructs Peter to "let down your nets for a catch" (Luke 5:4). It is highly unusual because the nets are designed for night fishing and it is already broad daylight. Being a professional fisherman, Peter objects to the seemingly senseless command. However, in the end he relents, "*But* because you say so, I will let down the nets" (verse 5, NIV; emphasis added). And a miracle happens—they catch so many fish that their nets begin to break and the boats start to sink.

Oh, what an experience, what a miracle of God! To be made so successful that the very tools of your trade, whatever it may be, start breaking! Actually it must be rather scary because the success seems to be so explosive, especially in contrast with the fact that previously, in the absence of Jesus, your efforts were fruitless. That is the whole point of this aspect of the narrative. Your success does not depend on your tools and definitely not on your skills and know-how. Instead it depends entirely on the presence and action of Jesus Christ. In my life and ministry sometimes I've had to learn this lesson the hard way. It's so easy to slip into an "I can" mentality, telling God, "I am the professional; I can handle this one by myself." But these are the times that usually precede our biggest failures and then we learn to depend on Him.

Having experienced this amazing demonstration of power that has no other explanation than God's intervention it suddenly dawns on Peter that he is in the presence of the Divine. And in God's presence his own sinfulness becomes unbearably obvious to him and an almost imperceptible whisper escapes his lips, "Go away from me Lord, for I am a sinful man!" (verse 8).

Radical Discipleship

This is a moment of great internal conflict. Because of his sinfulness, Peter feels totally unworthy to be in the presence of Jesus, yet that very Presence is the only thing that can cleanse his sin, so he falls at Jesus' feet. I am not worthy, but I need you! I am a sinful man, but please don't ever leave me! This is how in the palpable presence of Jesus a heart is transformed and reborn by the power of His love and grace. This is the place where the sinner can finally be himself and abandon the need to pretend to be better than he really is, fully trusting in the saving grace of God. Significantly, this is the place where Jesus calls His first disciples to transition from catching fish to catching men in order to help others enter the presence of Jesus, to have the same transformational experience of His love.

In John 21 we find the second part of the *inclusio*, where a similar story is recorded. Here, just like in Luke's narrative, the disciples have been laboring all night in vain but at the command of Jesus have such an enormous catch that they "[are] not able to haul it in because of the great number of fish" (verse 6). Once again, Jesus reminds them, and us, that He is the only One able to bring about the miraculous catch, whether of fish or humans.

Jesus did not choose these ordinary, flawed people by mistake. He was well aware of the monumental choice He was making, and He did not have cold feet about it the morning after. He chose these ordinary people for an unparalleled task because He was, and is, an extraordinary God! And He chose you too, as ordinary as you may feel. After all, radical discipleship is ordinary people *accepting* EXTRA-ordinary grace!

INDIVIDUAL OR SMALL GROUP STUDY QUESTIONS

1. Why did Jesus choose disciples?
2. What qualified the twelve disciples to be chosen by Jesus?
3. How does extraordinary grace apply to us today?
4. When is a person considered a disciple of Jesus?
5. What was Jesus teaching the disciples, and us, through the two fishing miracles at the beginning and end of His public ministry?

Chapter 2

EXTRA-Ordinary Forgiveness

My parents and my older siblings have told me that when I was little, I always had creative but somewhat crazy ideas. When I was given a chore, I would first try to invent an "easier way" of doing it. I often ended up building weird "helpful devices" for the job. Once, when I had to carry firewood to the shed, I came up with a "brilliant invention" by stretching a wire from a tree to the shed and hooking a bucket to the wire so that the wood could be "transported" to the shed instead of me having to carry it. Well, did I tell you that most of the time (read: always) my devices failed, which did not stop me from inventing new ones? And my devices were not always mechanical; sometimes they came in the form of rushed ideas.

Springtime was always the most difficult time to stay in school, especially the last few days, when summer break was so close, yet it felt so far. On one spring morning, when birds were chirping and the trees had the first green, it felt like torture to have to go to school. It was the last day of school, and I remember the wheels in my mind spinning fast as a new "device" was being invented. We typically had our textbooks on loan from the school library. And in my young mind I somehow imagined that if we did not have the text books, the teacher would simply let us go home early. I still don't understand how I managed to convince the whole class to return their textbooks back to the library, but I did. So when the teacher walked into the classroom, we were all smiles and happily informed her that since we did not have our textbooks we should just go home! Well, you can imagine how this one went down. It did not take long for the teacher to figure out who the instigator was. I not only received the scornful wrath of my peers for authoring this silly idea but also went home with a serious note to my parents. Once again I had rushed in with my invention and got burned.

This is how we meet Peter: full of ideas, trigger happy—an epitome of the Wild West principle of shoot first and ask questions later, philosophically speaking, that is. He is the one character among the disciples who

Radical Discipleship

is depicted most vividly and painted in the most vibrant colors. Peter is a man who never hesitates, who believes in quick action; even if it turns out to be the wrong action. Sound familiar? Before we go on, let's get to know him a bit more.

SO, WHO WAS THIS PETER?

Peter was an ordinary person who became obsessed with the extraordinary grace of God. And God was able to use him powerfully as a fearless leader, but not before he had experienced his own powerlessness through a major failure and had accepted the extraordinary forgiveness that allowed God's grace to invade and transform his heart.

Peter's original name was Simon. When Simon met Jesus, he got a new name, Peter (*Petros* in Greek, see Matthew 10:2), which means "stone" or "rock." The equivalent of Peter in Aramaic is *Cephas* (John 1:42). It must have been quite interesting for Peter to be called Rock or Stone (it seems to fit because he was really hardheaded). In Matthew 16:13–20 Peter made one of the most profound confessions about Jesus, "You are the Christ, the Son of the living God" (verse 16), after which Jesus made an important statement, "Blessed are you, Simon Barjona, because flesh and blood did not *reveal* this to you, but My Father who is in heaven. I also say to you that you are Peter [*Petros*], and upon *this* rock [*petra*] I will build My church" (verses 17, 18; emphasis added). This announcement has sometimes been misunderstood by some as if Jesus were talking about Peter as the rock on which He would build His church. Wow! What an honor to be *that* Rock! Right? But not so fast, Peter! You are not the main rock! It is the *revelation* that you just received! It is "the Christ, the Son of the living God" whom you have just confessed. *He* is the Rock on which the church is built. No confusion here!

PETER: A FAILING DISCIPLE!

In Mark 14 we find Jesus having the last meal together with His disciples, during which Jesus makes a stunning announcement: the disciples will *all fall away* (verse 27)! Peter jumps up and declares with burning passion and conviction that even though the others might fall away, he would never ever, not even in his wildest dreams, do that! Poor Peter is absolutely convinced about his moral character and his ability to exercise his willpower to stand up for Jesus. But Jesus turns to him and, in painful detail, outlines the way Peter would deny Him three times that night. But Peter still does not get it! "Even if I have to die with You, I will not deny You" (verse 31). Jesus, don't You know me better than that? I am Peter, the Rock! Remember, You gave me that name, doesn't it mean anything? I understand, the others may be weak, but it's me, Peter, I have been so loyal to You all along!

It's hard to imagine how Peter must have felt later that evening after his bravado and willpower had folded like a house of cards! Asked a simple question by a little servant girl, Peter had a chance to use his willpower, to say the right thing, but he wouldn't, he couldn't! He had not really known himself! His resolve had strangely disappeared, his willpower had dissolved, and he found himself swearing "I don't know this man you're talking about" (verse 71, NLT).

Luke 22:61 gives a very important detail about what happened after Peter's denial—Jesus looked him straight in the eyes. I try to imagine what Peter read in that brief glance of Jesus. Was it anger, or disdain, or perhaps bitterness? I don't believe Peter saw any of that. Instead, he saw the unconditional love of Christ, the love that had not been affected by his betrayal, the love that had not been diminished by his shameful rejection. That was the extraordinary love of the Son of God that, at this pivotal juncture, was invading Peter's heart. And out of that divine intervention, from the broken pieces of Peter's shattered life, a new man was born.

IS THERE MINISTRY AFTER FAILURE?

I am *so* glad you asked! After the Resurrection Jesus finds Peter at the lakeside with nets in hand. Once again he had worked all night but has caught nothing. And once again Jesus miraculously causes him to catch an incredibly great abundance of fish (John 21). This is almost an identical situation to the one narrated by Luke at the beginning of Jesus' ministry (Luke 5), which we analyzed in the previous chapter. Only this time Peter is a broken man, his reliance on self is gone, and his boasting about his heroic standing up for Jesus has vanished. Peter finally knows that he is really a sinful man, desperately needing God's grace. Peter has come full circle to the same place where three and a half years earlier he had acknowledged that he was a sinful man. This time the realization goes way deeper because he knows a little bit better what he is made of. But

Radical Discipleship

most important he knows what Jesus is made of.

Jesus has made a campfire and is inviting Peter, with his companions, to join Him. Just as Peter has denied Jesus three times, now Jesus gives Peter an opportunity to affirm his love three times. Oh, what a different Peter we see here! He is sad and hurt because of his sin, his self-reliance is completely gone. No, we do not hear what we are used to hearing from Peter. He does not say, "Jesus, how can You doubt me? Don't You know better? Of course, I love You!" No, that boastful Peter is gone, instead he humbly says, "You know that I love You" (John 21:15). And immediately Jesus reinstalls Peter into his calling to "feed my sheep" (verse 17, NIV).

Whenever I think of Peter, I remember myself and my own "devices," and my rushed judgment about my own abilities and the situations I have been in—not only in my childhood. There have also been plenty of those later in my life. There have been so many times when I was determined to stand for Jesus, to do the right thing, but I did not; I could not, because I did not know myself and my willpower just folded, and my resolve dissipated. But by God's grace, at the intersection of my own sinfulness and His extraordinary love and grace, I find His extraordinary forgiveness and a renewed commission: "Feed My sheep."

INDIVIDUAL OR SMALL GROUP STUDY QUESTIONS

1. Why is God's extraordinary forgiveness so pivotal for us as disciples of Jesus?
2. How does God redirect the zeal of passionate followers for *His glory*?
3. I easily identify with Peter on many levels. Do you? If yes, how?
4. Do you believe in your heart that "there is ministry after failure" when you have tasted Jesus' extraordinary forgiveness?
5. Why do you think Peter was so sure of himself before he failed miserably? Can the same happen to us?

CHAPTER 3

EXTRA-Ordinary Love

When I was about ten years old, I used to play with the neighbors' kids. We generally got along quite well, except when we didn't. Those episodes, however, could become quite intense as we fought our verbal battles to the bitter end. One of those experiences has stuck in my mind forever, not because of what we were fighting about, but because of what I said. Since I grew up in a devout Christian family, I was taught to use every opportunity to share my faith with others. And somehow this quarrel seemed an opportune moment not only to declare my faith in God but also to use God as a weapon to get even. So in the heat of the argument, as I was running out of good comebacks, I decided to throw in my religion and declared with all the force of my ten-year-old conviction, "Do you know that God will burn you in fire because you are so bad to me?"

Somehow I am pretty sure that my "missionary venture" did not convert anybody. However, the truth is that I sometimes catch myself doing the same thing even now as a grown-up, in a much more subtle way, of course. And I suspect I am not alone in this. Let's take a look at another disciple who struggled with the same type of "evangelistic tactic."

BUT JESUS' DISCIPLES ALWAYS BEHAVE WELL, DON'T THEY?

Not really. Jesus had a disciple who had such a short fuse that He gave him, along with his brother, a special nickname—*boanerges*—"sons of thunder" (Mark 3:17). Yes, John was an angry man, quick to judge and with a short temper. In a story found in Luke 9:51–55, we see Jesus, on a tiresome journey toward Jerusalem, desiring to stop over at a small Samaritan village. However, the villagers are not very hospitable to Jesus. John becomes so angry and upset that he, just like me during my childhood, comes up with a quick solution—the destruction of the unwelcoming people, "Lord, do You want us to command fire to come down from heaven and consume them?" (verse 54). John

Radical Discipleship

must have been a really angry man indeed.

John and his brother James grew up in a fisherman's family in the town of Capernaum. Their father, Zebedee, owned a fishing business and seemed to have been in partnership with the family of Peter and Andrew (Luke 5:10). Both sets of siblings became close followers of Jesus. On one occasion he and James approached Jesus privately with an exclusive request about being given the two top positions in His coming kingdom (Mark 10:35–45). The brothers had hoped that this conversation would remain a secret, but it turns out that the other disciples overheard their bold request and were not happy about it. "Hearing this, the ten began to feel *indignant* with James and John" (verse 41; emphasis added). I can see why, can't you? It seemed as though Jesus had more than enough reasons to reject John as a disciple. But He didn't.

JESUS' OUTRAGEOUS CHOICE

Given these unflattering characteristics of self-seeking and uncontrollable anger, one would think that John probably did not amount to much and that Jesus could not really use him to communicate His gospel of love. Jesus surely could not have any use for angry people; he could not have invited a "rageaholic" like John to be His representative. If you think so, think again! You are in for quite a surprise.

Astonishingly, John distinguishes himself in the Gospels in a unique and totally unexpected way. There is something about him that sets him apart from all the others, and it is not the fact that he becomes one of the most influential church leaders. John is known by a very special and unique relationship with Jesus, his all-stops-pulled-out, uninhibited, absolute commitment to the love of Jesus. And so, surprisingly, John goes down in history as the disciple of love. How is that possible, we wonder! The angry, irrational, hot-headed man, known as the disciple of love?

John never mentions his own name in his Gospel, instead he always refers to himself as "the disciple whom Jesus loved" (John 13:23; 19:26; 21:7; 21:20, NIV). Why does he do that? It is abundantly clear throughout the biblical narrative that Jesus loves all of His disciples equally, even Judas, the traitor. He loves you and me, in spite of our problems, be it anger or anything else! But why the notable difference in John? John chooses to really believe in the love of Jesus and accept it. That extraordinary love becomes John's hallmark, his signature, his banner, his guiding principle that permeates his life and ministry. The usage of the word *love* in the Gospels makes the point—Matthew uses the word seventeen times; Mark, eight times; and Luke, nineteen times. However, John uses the word *love* fifty-seven times in his Gospel and fifty-two times in his letters. Some of his statements on love are very well known, such as John 3:16 and 1 John 3:1. Can you imagine? One hundred and nine occurrences of the word *love* in his writings! He is literally obsessed with Jesus' love! That explains why Jesus chooses Peter to "feed His sheep" but John to take care of His mother (John 19:26, 27).

THE BELOVED DISCIPLE

Before His death on the cross, Jesus has one last meal with His disciples. As they are reclining on pillows on the floor, around a U-shaped low table (a typical scene of first-century Palestine), Jesus catches His friends and companions totally by surprise with His shocking announcement that one of them will become a traitor (John 13). Since John is reclining next to Jesus, Peter gives him a sign to find out specifics on the issue (verses 23, 24). The Gospel describes the situation, "*Leaning back thus on Jesus' bosom*, [John] said to Him, 'Lord, who is it?' " (verse 25; emphasis added). We can imagine how John was leaning toward Jesus in order to whisper the question privately in His ear, and how he must have felt the heartbeat of Jesus. It is true that heart speaks to heart. There was a soul connection that John constantly sought with Jesus. Yes, he was an angry man, but he relentlessly sought the presence of Jesus, constantly listened to His heartbeat, and immersed himself in His love. The EXTRA-ordinary love of Jesus had broken through the defenses of anger of this ordinary man.

John, who had started his journey with Jesus as an ordinary, angry, and self-seeking man, accepted Jesus' extraordinary love and came to call himself "the one whom Jesus loves," because he dared to believe that Jesus really did love him. He never looked at himself primarily as a disciple, a pastor, an apostle, or anything else related to what he was doing. He was consistently the one whom Jesus loved, the continuous recipient of His extraordinary love. That was his real self, his identity, his motivation to work for Christ, and his source of strength and courage in his trials—he was the one Jesus loved. That love animated his life, motivated his ministry,

Radical Discipleship

and was the core of his message to this world. This was not a message that he had learned from a book or in a school, this was the message borne out of his real-life experience with Jesus—being the one Jesus loved.

You are the beloved of the Lord!

If you were called a son or daughter of thunder, do you think you would qualify for the label? Given my early "missionary activities," and similar experiences later in my life, I definitely would. So often I find myself rushing to judgment without compassion for others! Even though most of the time the battle takes place in my mind, it's still real! Just get me on a freeway in the fast lane behind somebody driving below the speed limit! If only you could read my thoughts! Talk about a short fuse, huh? If you understand what I am talking about, John would tell you—"Welcome to the club, friend!" And no, this is not a group of irritated, annoying folks who want to vent their anger. John is inviting us into a fellowship of ordinary, and in many ways flawed, people who have realized their brokenness and have discovered the extraordinary love Jesus has for them. This is the club of ex-*boanerges,* the gathering of sons and daughters of thunder who are being drawn by the incredible grace and love of Jesus; these are *the people whom Jesus loves.* Welcome to the club, friend!

Individual or Small Group Study Questions

1. How does Jesus' extraordinary love take us from *grudge* to *grace*?
2. Why is love a much stronger motivator than fear?
3. How does Jesus' choice of John as a disciple affect your life today?
4. Why do you think John became so passionate about Jesus' love?
5. Mention some of your favorite verses where John mentions *love.*

Chapter 4

EXTRA-Ordinary Revelation

I have a sister who is two years older and a brother who is four years older than me. As the three of us were growing up in Latvia, my sister had a motherly type of personality (she still has it today) always taking care of me and defending me when I got in trouble. My personality, however, was somewhat less nurturing. As a matter of fact, I frequently found myself fighting for "my rights," which often appeared threatened by my older brother.

In Latvia most people relied on public transportation in those days. My dad, however, purchased a motorcycle with a sidecar which was a huge step up as a means of family transportation. This is how it worked: my mother rode on the motorcycle behind my dad and the three of us kids got tucked into the sidecar, my older brother facing forward and my sister and I facing backward. In addition, my dad had built a contraption over the sidecar, covered with tarp, to protect us from the elements. There was even a plastic "windshield" in the front through which my brother (not me, mind you) could peek at the road. Thus, all five of us fit into the vehicle and were able to travel around for the amusement of other people who seemed to have never seen a sight like that.

The problem was, however, that my older brother always got the front seat. I complained, "Why is it that he always gets to sit in the front and watch the road? It's not fair." It was a privilege, and I wanted a piece of it too! Never mind that given our different ages and sizes this configuration was the only way our parents could get us all in. That's how my transportation angst began. But it did not end there. By the time we graduated from the motorcycle to a tiny car with an air-cooled engine in the back, my brother and I had also graduated from the problem of who got to sit facing forward (we all could sit facing forward now) to who got to sit in the driver's seat. Even though neither of us was old enough to have a driver's license, we both coveted the prize of driving the car the last few hundred yards from the main road to our house. By the way, I wasn't

Radical Discipleship

even tall enough to see over the steering wheel, so I drove the car peering through the gap between the dashboard and the top of the steering wheel. Whenever the family was returning home, the two of us would have a spirited argument about who should get to drive the car over that little stretch of the dirt road.

It's curious that this kind of striving for the best seat or best place, whatever that may happen to be, is not limited only to boys growing up in rural areas; it affects everyone. Really! It even affected the disciples of Jesus!

WHO GETS THE BEST SEAT?

That's where we meet James (Mark 10:35–45), together with his brother John, trying to outsmart the other disciples in their race to the best "seats" in the kingdom of Jesus. James occupied a significant position among the disciples; he was consistently mentioned in the first group, the intimate circle. He was one of Jesus' closest confidants and accompanied Him in the most important and difficult times of His life. Being in the group as one of the three disciples closest to Jesus (Peter, James, and John), James got to see firsthand, extraordinary revelations that the others hadn't experience. For example James saw the resurrection of Jairus' daughter (Luke 8:51–56), the transfiguration of Jesus and the supernatural encounter with Moses and Elijah, and he heard the very *voice* of God! (Luke 9:28–36). And he had many other extraordinary revelations of Jesus! You would think that experiencing the supernatural firsthand would humble him, right? Well, that's not what happened to James. It did influence him quite a bit, but in a different way: it got to his head! Perhaps it would have gotten to my head as well. When you get into a privileged position, it has a way of turning your ego on. All of a sudden you start feeling important, powerful, and indispensable, and you get the thirst for even more importance and power. You need to be in the driver's seat, like my brother and I.

Let's go back to Mark 10:35–45. Jesus is on His final journey to Jerusalem, where He would lay down His life to secure salvation for humanity. Yet, all of His disciples seem to be preoccupied with their expectations that Jesus would soon restore the throne of King David, which would naturally come with certain perks and privileges for *them*. They are thinking about the high government positions that they deserve. *Oh, there is so much "perceived" power in being close to Jesus that I can start craving for*

Him—not to have Him in my life but just to get the perks. Now that Jesus is going to Jerusalem, the disciples are getting really excited, thinking that their cherished goal is just around the corner. Finally, they will be able to transition from a ragtag band of nobodies to members of the new government, to move right into the driver's seat. They think Jesus is about to begin filling the key positions in the new government, never mind that He constantly has pointed to His impending suffering and death. As they approach Jerusalem, James' urgency turns feverish. *This is the moment!* he thinks. *I've got to get into the driver's seat. I've been so close to Jesus, I deserve it!*

You want what?

James and John decide to beat everyone else to it and come to Jesus privately, "Grant that we may sit, one on Your right and one on Your left, in Your glory" (Mark 10:37). Remember the honor social system, in which dinner guests would be seated according to their place in the social hierarchy? There were three top spots reserved at the table—one for the host and one to his right and the other to his left. Therefore, what James (and John) are actually doing here is claiming for themselves the very top positions in the government of Jesus. They are really shooting for the moon!

Way to go, James! This is how you get ahead in life. You've got to climb the ladder to the very top. Reach for the stars! This is the way the world works, and you have to work the pecking order. If you don't take care of yourself, who else will? You don't want to spend your whole life in the back—move on to the driver's seat, right?

Jesus' response, however, was not exactly what James expected, "You don't know what you are asking. Are you able to drink the cup that I drink, or to be baptized with the baptism with which I am baptized?" (verse 38). While James was thinking about the kingdom in terms of honor, rank, and being in the driver's seat, Jesus was talking about it in terms of His glory through His suffering on the cross. Significantly, the same phrase "one on his right and one on his left" is used later (Mark 15:27, NIV) to describe those crucified with Jesus, thus turning James's concept of glory on its head. Being close to Jesus does not always bring the perks of an earthly kingdom, but it does mean participating in His

Radical Discipleship

kingdom and His suffering. Ironically, James did get to "drink from the cup." His martyrdom is recorded in Acts 12:2.

Oh, James, it was a brilliant plan. But that's not how Jesus' kingdom works! And it did not take long for the others to figure out what that private conversation was all about (Mark 10:41). I can still remember the wrath of my brother after I had managed to privately convince my father that it was my turn to drive! I kept hearing about it for a very, very long time. The firestorm that erupted was so bad that Jesus had to intervene and set the matter straight. He told them, "You know that those who are recognized as rulers of the Gentiles *lord it over* them; and their great men *exercise authority* over them. But *it is not this way among you*, but whoever wishes to become great among you shall be your servant" (verses 42, 43; emphasis added).

THE SERVANT LEADER

Jesus is saying that in His kingdom things are radically different. The word *Gentiles* depicts the way of this world, whose dominating principle is the survival of the fittest, where the strong and the powerful rule over the weak and the insignificant. The two concepts—*rule over* and *exercise authority*—are translated from Greek compound verbs, both beginning with *kata*, meaning "down." This reflects how this world functions—by pushing others down in order to climb the ladder and advance through the pecking order that permeates our society on all levels, including state, business, academia, church, and even playground.

But Jesus represents a diametrically different order. He says, "But it is not this way among you, but whoever wishes to become great among you shall be your *servant*; and whoever wishes to be first among you shall be *slave* of all" (verses 43, 44; emphasis added). A servant (Greek *diakonos*) performed household duties and was serving others instead of himself. A slave (Greek *doulos*) was someone bound to obey the master, not free to do as he wishes. Both *diakonos* and *doulos* were at the bottom of the pecking order. Jesus is making it abundantly clear that whoever has an ambition to be in service to God must serve others. Under God's rule, those who are last will be first. James had to understand that his preoccupation with rank and significance had no place in God's kingdom.

Jesus demonstrated His answer to James in His own life, "For even the Son of Man did not come to be served, but to serve, and to give His life a ransom for many" (verse 45). Jesus was willing to abandon everything in order to serve and redeem us. He died in our place, substituting His life for ours! That puts things in perspective, doesn't it? Could it be that the secret of true greatness is not found in perks nor getting into the driver's seat, but in service to others and, thus, found in Jesus? This is the extraordinary revelation captured in His life and death.

Anytime someone who claims to be close to Jesus gets proud, critical, and self-seeking, you know that this person is very far from God! The closer you get to the Master, and the more you accept of the extraordinary revelation of the gospel of Jesus Christ, the more sinful and undeserving you will feel. The disciple of Jesus is an ordinary person who has accepted the extraordinary revelation of the good news of Jesus Christ and lives in *awe* of His grace! We invite you to join us; we are the awe-stricken-undeserving-and-yet-saved-by-grace disciples of Jesus!

INDIVIDUAL OR SMALL GROUP STUDY QUESTIONS

1. List several situations in which Jesus took *only* Peter, James, and John with Him.
2. Why do you think Jesus chose to have a closer inner group from among the disciples (Peter, James, and John)?
3. Why are human beings in danger of becoming proud when God gives them extraordinary revelations of His grace? (See 2 Corinthians 12:7.)
4. What does Mark 10:45 mean to you personally?
5. Please respond to this definition of discipleship: Discipleship is a reversal of values in light of the Cross.

Chapter 5

EXTRA-Ordinary Master

Several years ago I was at the Bugema University in Uganda to teach a few graduate intensive courses. While there I met a young student whom I will never forget. I spent a while with him, sitting on a bench in the middle of the campus, as he shared with me his story. Just a few months earlier, Geoffrey (this is not his real name) had purchased a ticket to fly to Pakistan. On the morning of his flight he discovered his passport missing and began frantically looking for it. However, he could not find it. As time passed, he became more and more desperate, and he ended up missing his flight. Geoffrey was so angry that he did not want to see anybody, yet he bumped into a young man who was excited and eager to talk. Ignoring Geoffrey's grumpiness, he tried to strike up a conversation with him. This young man was a Christian, so excited about Jesus that he simply had to tell everybody about his Master. Geoffrey would not hear about it. And yet, as the young man persisted, Geoffrey gradually started listening, and the words sank in and strangely began to make sense. Deep down Geoffrey started to like what he was hearing, and before long a miracle happened and he fell in love with Jesus. Now, just four months later, the two of us were meeting at a Christian university where Geoffrey was a ministerial student preparing to witness for his new Master, Jesus Christ. God was able to use that ordinary young Christian man to introduce his extraordinary Master to Geoffrey! The day when he missed his flight, Geoffrey was heading to a terrorist camp where he had planned to enroll to train for a suicide mission.

BEHIND-THE-SCENES DISCIPLE

Among the disciples Andrew stands out with this same kind of simple witness to his extraordinary Master. Even though he and his brother Peter, together with James and John, belong to the first group of four in the apostolic hierarchy, he seems to always remain in the shadow of the others.

EXTRA-Ordinary Master

And indeed he is mostly a behind-the-scenes guy—not one who receives recognition for thousands of baptisms; not one known as a spectacular preacher, drawing great crowds.

Andrew, with his brother Simon Peter, grew up by the Sea of Galilee in the town of Bethsaida in the family of their father, Jonah or John (Matthew 16:17; John 1:42). Later on they both lived in Capernaum where Peter owned a house (Mark 1:29). Andrew and Peter were fishermen (Matthew 4:18) and seem to have been business partners with John and James, the sons of Zebedee (Luke 5:10).

Early on in his life Andrew was convicted by the preaching of John the Baptist and chose to follow him as his master. But, unlike other preachers of the time who were interested in their own following, John kept pointing to another One who would come after him and be infinitely greater than himself (John 1:30). Andrew soon caught John's passion for Jesus and, together with another disciple, decided to seek to know Him better (verse 40). They spent a day with Jesus, and that was enough for Andrew to become convinced that Jesus was indeed the Messiah. Without hesitation he joined Him and became His disciple (verses 35–40).

And here is the wonderful thing about Andrew: he was so thrilled about having found his extraordinary Master that he could not stay silent. He had to go and share it with someone else. Immediately he started looking for his brother Simon (Peter) in order to introduce him to Jesus (verses 41, 42). Can you imagine Andrew in his overflowing joy running around breathlessly calling out, "Simon! Simon! Where are you?" In his excitement and urgency he asks people on the street, "Have you seen Simon? Tell me where he is. I need to find him!" When, totally out of breath, he finally stumbles upon Simon Peter on the beach, all he can muster is, "We found Him! We found Him!"

"What? Whom did you find?" Simon asks, quite confused.

"The most extraordinary Master, the *Messiah*! We've found the Christ! Can you believe it?"

"He brought him to Jesus," are the words John uses to conclude the story (verse 42). Oh, how I love these simple words bursting with the joy of salvation! And what a real thrill it is to be in Andrew's shoes and lead people to Jesus! There is nothing even close to the delight that comes from leading a person to Jesus.

Radical Discipleship

TRUSTING THE EXTRAORDINARY MASTER

Andrew's character and trust in Jesus come to light more distinctly in the Gospel of John, chapter 6, where the disciples are facing the challenge of finding food for a great multitude of people. First, Jesus turns to Philip with a rhetorical question, "Where are we to buy bread, so that these may eat?" (verse 5). Philip, however, understands the question literally, and responds accordingly, "Two hundred denarii worth of bread is not sufficient for them, for everyone to receive a little!" (verse 7). In other words, Philip pulls out a calculator and attempts to prove that in order to feed this many people, they would need an enormous amount of money.

Andrew approaches the issue from a totally different perspective, however. Where others see only a crowd he sees individual people, so he spots a little boy who has a lunch box with him that contains a very small amount of food in it—five bite-sized barley buns and two tiny fish. This was the typical staple of the poor. Amazingly, by focusing on his extraordinary Master, Andrew is able to see beyond the impossibility of the situation. He brings the boy to Jesus, having a hunch that He just might be able to do something with the minuscule amount of food. Yet, his hunch and his faith are not a denial of the facts, so just in case, and in order not to look like a fool; he adds a vague question, "But what are these for so many people?" (verse 9).

But Jesus does not need a sufficient amount of resources in order to accomplish His goal. He turns this badly insufficient amount of ordinary food, offered by the simple boy, into an extraordinary feast for thousands of hungry people. According to Matthew's version of this event (Matthew 14:19), Jesus takes the little food available, gives thanks, breaks the bread, and gives it to the disciples to hand to the people. What a feast that must have been! There really was plenty of food and it was not rationed—it's not as though everybody received just a crumb of bread and perhaps a fish tail. No, everybody ate "as much as they wanted" (John 6:11). John makes sure we understand how plentiful the food was by informing the reader that there were twelve baskets of leftovers gathered after the meal! Can you imagine starting with a mere lunch box and ending up fully feeding five thousand men (plus many more women and children!) and then having the leftovers exceed the original resources by twelve baskets? In an instant they had gone from empty hands to a scrumptious feast, from laughably little resources to a multitude fed and satisfied with leftovers exceeding the initial resources a hundredfold. How crazy great is that?

FROM SCARCITY TO ABUNDANCE!

Andrew had truly lived his God-given purpose in this situation. He knew his extraordinary Master, he noticed the boy, he brought him to Jesus—and the miracle happened! He did not have to conduct a series of evangelistic meetings, he did not have to be a great speaker, and he did not even have to interact with the crowd. All he needed to do for this incredible miracle to happen was to notice one ordinary person and bring him to his extraordinary Master.

God is a liberal and generous giver. When we reach out to that person whom God calls us to bring to Jesus, we do not have to worry about if we have enough wisdom to convince her or if we have enough oratorial skills to communicate with him. We will have more and above what is needed. Jesus said, about those of us who are willing to choose faith instead of a calculator, "They will pour into your lap a good measure—pressed down, shaken together, and running over" (Luke 6:38).

And this applies to our salvation and everyday life as well. You might wake up one morning and realize that you don't have what it takes to make it, whether in your spiritual life, marriage, work, school, or ministry. God is not waiting for our ability, but for our availability. He will supply what is needed and will turn nothingness into abundance, because that's how it works in the kingdom of God: ordinary people accepting extraordinary grace from an extraordinary Master.

I will never forget Geoffrey, the suicide bomber wannabe, at Bugema University, a living testimony to our extraordinary Master who could take the limited ability of that young Christian man, who decided to obey the call of God, to be His witness in that situation no matter the odds. The abundance of results from his witness is impossible to comprehend, not until eternity reveals it! I can't wait to see the real impact of this miracle—the extraordinary surplus of "twelve basketfuls" of souls redeemed by Jesus, our extraordinary Master.

Radical Discipleship
INDIVIDUAL OR SMALL GROUP STUDY QUESTIONS

1. Are you comfortable being an "Andrew" instead of a "Peter"?
2. Why do you think that Andrew became so passionate about sharing his extraordinary, newfound Master?
3. What does the miraculous feeding teach us about our salvation?
4. Can God utilize any disciple who is willing to trust Him?
5. Read Romans 8:28. Do you believe that this extraordinary Master can turn all things (not just five loaves of bread) to the good of those who love Him?

CHAPTER 6

EXTRA-Ordinary Insight

"To be loved but not known is comforting but superficial. To be known and not loved is our greatest fear. But to be fully known and truly loved is . . . like being loved by God. It is what we need more than anything," reflects Timothy Keller in his book *The Meaning of Marriage*.[1] I remember learning the meaning of this thought at a rather early age, through fear of being found out and through my mother's unconditional love in the face of the ugliness of my sin.

When I was in grade school, we lived about a mile and a half from the school, and each day I walked to school by myself (at that time it was considered perfectly safe). After school sometimes I was allowed to walk a half mile farther to a little town to purchase a cone of ice cream which was a treat to die for. I remember a time when I was totally broke, with not a penny to my soul, but with desperate cravings for ice cream (by the way, I still get those sometimes). I realized that desperate times called for desperate measures as I considered my options and came up with a plan. In the evening, when everybody was out of the front room, I snuck into the closet and started going through the pockets of everybody's coats. It almost took my breath away when I discovered a large silver coin in my dad's pocket. Wow, I remember the thrill of my find and how I was trying to decide what to do! If I took the coin, would Dad notice? If he did, I would be in deep trouble. But he might not notice, he might even not remember having the coin in his pocket! But I also knew that I was about to cross a line that I had never crossed before—becoming a thief—and that troubled me a lot. Yet, my cravings for ice cream prevailed and I took the coin. I don't remember how I bought the ice cream or if I enjoyed it at all. But I do remember the devastating guilt I experienced about becoming a thief and the fear that my theft would be discovered. These emotions haunted me for days.

One evening as I was going to bed my mom sat down to pray with me and to tuck me in. She had been sensing the struggle that was raging in

Radical Discipleship

my heart and wanted to remind me how much Jesus loved me and how He died for me—how He promised never ever to abandon me. Oh, how I longed to get rid of the guilt and fear that had tormented me for so long! In my anxiety I blurted out a question: "If someone does something bad, will Jesus still love him?" My mother paused for a moment and then whispered in the gentlest way, "Honey, I know about the silver coin, and I love you nonetheless! And Jesus loves you even more!" First of all this insight came as a tremendous shock that rocked my whole world, and then it unplugged a whole dam that had been holding back my emotions and they started to flow freely, with plenty of tears and words of contrition: "I am so sorry. I do not want to steal. I don't understand what happened! Can you forgive me?"

My mother tried to help me grasp the new reality, the only thing that could restore my broken heart—I was loved unconditionally, regardless of what I had done. "You don't have to be afraid—I love you and always will. I will never stop loving you. You need to know that stealing hurts, first of all yourself; however, I love you regardless." That was my first encounter with someone knowing my darkness and still loving me. Later in my life God gave me opportunities to relive similar experiences all over again, but on a much deeper level, thus transforming my life by His love.

You know me?

Nathanael is introduced to us by John as a disciple whom Jesus knows. In the narrative, recorded in John 1:43–51, we first meet Philip who is so excited about the newfound Messiah that he immediately goes to find Nathanael and blurts out a whole lot of information in one breath, "We have found Him of whom Moses in the Law and also the prophets wrote—Jesus of Nazareth, the son of Joseph" (verse 45). Hey, Philip—not so fast, slow down a bit! Nathanael is in no way a gullible man; he will not be easily persuaded. It is a bit too much information for Nathanael, and he gets stuck on some deeply seated prejudice against Nazareth. Philip forgoes the theological debate and makes a simple invitation, "Come and see" (verse 46), to which Nathanael has no objection. He meets Jesus, and his life will never be the same again.

Before Nathanael even arrives, Jesus depicts him in a fascinating manner. He says, "Behold, an Israelite indeed, in whom there is no deceit!"

(verse 47). The Greek word, translated here as "deceit," is *dolos*, and it is defined as "taking advantage through craft and underhanded methods, deceit, cunning, treachery."[2] The listeners of Jesus and the readers of John must have been familiar with this usage of the word and therefore must have understood what Jesus was hinting at. Nathanael is an authentic person who does not pretend to be something other than what he really is. He is definitely no bait-and-switch person! Remember the Trojan horse that Greeks used to gain access to the city of Troy? Nathanael is not like that. You get what you see; there is nothing hidden, no need to read between the lines, no need to pretend to be better than you are.

And that is exactly how salvation works. I do not have to make myself look better than I really am. Why? Because, as I had learned in my childhood experience with my mom, God has an extraordinary insight; He knows the real me. I cannot shock Him, I cannot hide anything. But the most astounding thing about God is that, though knowing the real me (which is not always pretty), He still loves me. Our salvation does not depend on how we look but is received as a gift. The only ticket to the kingdom of God is the acceptance of that gift—no *dolos*, no fish bait, no spiritual makeup. Like a trusting child just accept the gift of salvation from the hands of your heavenly Parent, eyes filled with wonder and excitement.

Jesus reveals to Nathanael another insight about him, "Before Philip called you, when you were under the fig tree, I saw you" (verse 48). This awareness that Jesus has about Nathanael affects him profoundly. A short while ago he had responded to Philip quite arrogantly, but now all of a sudden he senses the presence of God. Now he realizes how trivial his earlier objections and prejudice have really been. *Amazingly, Jesus knows me! Just imagine—He knows me!* In response and from the bottom of his heart Nathanael exclaims, "Rabbi, You are the Son of God; You are the King of Israel" (verse 49). What an amazing change! A total turnaround, from deep skepticism and prejudice to perhaps the greatest confession of Jesus that anyone has ever made!

Significantly, at the end of the Gospel, Jesus is called the King once again, this time by Pilate, who places a notice on the cross, "JESUS THE NAZARENE, THE KING OF THE JEWS" (John 19:19). This is called an *inclusio*, a literary sandwich, that is used to make a point; and for added emphasis. Jesus is King and His Kingship is brought about through His sacrifice for you and me. He is our true King who lay down His life for His own (John 10:11).

THE HEAVENLY LADDER

It must be earth shattering for Nathanael to realize that Jesus knows his life. He reads it like an open book, all his secrets, all his flaws; and yet He does not reject him! Jesus says, "You shall see greater things than these. . . . You will see heaven opened, and the angels of God ascending and descending upon the Son of Man" (John 1:50, 51, RSV). Jesus refers here to the great master cheater, the skilled *dolos* practitioner, Jacob, who having stolen his brother's blessing was running for his life. He had a dream while staying overnight at Bethel (Genesis 28:10–15). Tormented by fear and guilt, Jacob saw a stairway reaching up to heaven and angels walking up and down. Jesus explains and expands upon the vision of Jacob. He Himself is the stairway that Jacob saw at Bethel who bridges the abyss between God and guilt-ridden humanity. The angels are ascending and descending on the Son of Man, the One who knows everything about us and yet loves us and gave up His life in order to save us. And thus, the extraordinary Master gives an extraordinary insight about His intimate knowledge and love for humankind!

My mother's unconditional love left an indelible impression on my young heart, tormented by guilt and fear. I was overwhelmed that she could know everything that I had done and still be kind to me and love me. I am so thankful to God for that childhood experience and for more profound experiences that awaited me later in life, when I was *so* aware of Him seeing and knowing everything about me—His ability to read my heart like a book. He knew all there was to know about me—even the worst secrets that I had tucked away in the darkness of my heart. It left me breathless and totally amazed that He still accepted me and loved me unconditionally. Those earth-shattering encounters were awe-inspiring and life-transforming experiences. And I have come to believe that such encounters with Jesus are where radical discipleship begins: His extraordinary insight into my heart accompanied by His extraordinary love for me.

EXTRA-Ordinary Insight
INDIVIDUAL OR SMALL GROUP STUDY QUESTIONS

1. How is it possible that those who study the Scriptures, like Nathanael, may also hold deep-seated prejudice like he did?
2. Why are we afraid of being fully known?
3. Respond to the extraordinary insight that there is nothing you can do that will make God love you less.
4. Mention other cases in the Gospels where people are transformed by finding themselves fully known and fully loved by Jesus.
5. What is the importance of Jesus revealing Himself as the mediating Stairway between heaven and earth?

---

1. Timothy Keller with Kathy Keller, *The Meaning of Marriage: Facing the Complexities of Commitment With the Wisdom of God,* reprint ed. (New York: Penguin Books, 2013), 101.

2. Frederick W. Danker, ed., *A Greek-English Lexicon of the New Testament and Other Early Christian Literature,* 3rd ed. (Chicago: University of Chicago Press, 2001), 256.

Chapter 7

EXTRA-Ordinary Acceptance

No one wants to experience rejection. Rejection causes fear; rejection engenders low self-worth and ultimately leads to self-hatred. As a kid I was never very athletic (not that I am very athletic now). I remember in physical education class, when we played team sports, the teacher usually would select two captains who would then take turns calling members for their respective teams. Everybody wanted to be chosen; I wanted to be chosen, I wanted to be wanted. But most of the time I ended up being the very last person selected, and it was painful to listen to the team captains arguing about me. "You take him," said one of them. "No, you take him. Remember, I took him last time," the other retorted. "No, I don't want to. He will ruin the game!" was the blunt response. And so it went on and on until the teacher took pity on me and assigned me to a team. Unfortunately by then it really did not feel much like acceptance at all. Rejection was hard for me to take and still is. Years later I discovered the extraordinary and amazing acceptance of God, in spite of my shortcomings and failures, and even in the face of my sin. And that extraordinary acceptance changed everything.

WHO WILL TAKE THAT ONE?

When Jesus called His disciples, there was one who knew exactly how it feels to be rejected. The Gospel of Matthew includes a narrative of Jesus calling Matthew, the tax collector (Matthew 9:9–13). The other two synoptic evangelists also describe the call of a tax collector and the subsequent dinner at his house, only they name him Levi.

Matthew is a prime example of a rejected person. In the first century, Palestine tax collection was a generally hated and despised occupation. First of all, these tax collectors (Greek *telones*) were considered traitors and turncoats because they collaborated with the enemy, the hated Romans. Second, the Romans had a very subjective system of collecting this type

EXTRA-Ordinary Acceptance

of tax. They did not like to collect it themselves, so they outsourced the job to the locals. It could be a very lucrative business because the trade was open to manipulation and fraud. The system permitted the agents to set their own, extremely high rates to line their pockets with the overage. People typically did not know what the rates were and were powerless in the hands of the unscrupulous tax collectors. This is where we find Levi Matthew, running his unethical but very lucrative business, when suddenly Jesus invades his life.

YES! YOU! FOLLOW ME!

"After that He went out and noticed a tax collector named Levi sitting in the tax booth, and He said to him, 'Follow Me.' And he left everything behind, and got up and began to follow Him" (Luke 5:27, 28). Jesus is really going out on a limb here, stepping way out of the accepted norms of propriety. What respectable rabbi would go and talk to a tax collector like that? It's unheard of! Where are Your manners, Jesus? Don't You know better than that? What example are You showing to the watching community by associating with this sinner? But Jesus does not care what others are thinking. He is a "Friend of sinners" and has come into this world specifically to accept the unacceptable, to accept all kinds of sinners, which include you and me.

Prior to meeting Jesus, Levi must have heard about Him, perhaps even watched Him heal a sick person or heard Him preach to the crowd. So he could have imagined accidentally meeting Jesus in a synagogue or seeing Him from a distance among the teachers of the law! But of all the places not here! Not at the place of his dirty business, where his little, grimy heart is bared for all to see. . . .

There is a line at his booth.

A fledgling merchant barely making ends meet to feed his wife and children wants to sell his wares in the city. The Roman tax is one denarius. Matthew demands three.

The poor man pays up, too timid to ask questions.

"Next!" Matthew motions to a fisherman with a basketful of the morning catch.

The Roman tax is half a denarius for fishermen. But this man

Radical Discipleship

can hardly count, so he stretches out his palm with a few coins; Matthew helps himself to two denarii.

"Next!" Matthew raises his head toward the waiting taxpayers and gets dumbstruck. "Rabbi, is that You? . . . What are *You* doing here? What are You doing *here*? Did You just see . . . what I . . . ?"

A wave of shame and self-condemnation wells over Matthew's heart and makes him want to sink into the ground. This must be the worst day of his life! The Great Teacher has just showed up and at the worst possible moment—to witness all his trickery. Matthew lowers his eyes in shame.

"Follow Me." He hears Jesus' cheerful voice and can't believe his ears.

"Jesus, are You talking to me? Really?!"

Once the words of Jesus have sunk in, there is not a moment of hesitation. The Bible says that Matthew "left everything and followed him" (verse 28, NIV). That is a whole lot to leave, but all of it seems useless now. In the presence of Jesus things are *so* different! All he wants now is Jesus!

COME! COME! MEET THE ONE!

Levi cannot contain his excitement about Jesus, so he puts together a banquet for his new Friend. "And Levi gave a big reception for Him in his house; and there was a great crowd of tax collectors and *other people* who were reclining *at the table* with them" (verse 29; emphasis added). The phrase "other people" implies that, apart from his tax collector buddies, he had also invited all kinds of outcasts and rejects—the kind of people nobody invites to parties.

The Pharisees are concerned and take the list of objectionable invitees to the disciples for clarification: "Why do you eat and drink with tax collectors and sinners?" (verse 30). Interestingly, Jesus does not try to be diplomatic here, nor does He even object to the Pharisee's claim that Levi's guests are despicable, because they are. He simply says, "It is not those who are well who need a physician, but those who are sick. I have not come to call the righteous but sinners to repentance." (verses 31, 32). He admits that these people are sick, they are sinners; but they have come to Jesus with nothing else but their great need, and He is going to show them nothing else but His extraordinary acceptance.

The Pharisees, on the other hand, feel they need nothing; they are well, they are good and righteous. And they cannot stand sin, not in others. But their problem is not that they cannot stand sin. They didn't even know that *they* are sinners! That's why Jesus says to the chief priests and elders, "The tax collectors and prostitutes will get into the kingdom of God before you" (Matthew 21:31). Tax collectors know their need; Pharisees and the religious elite not so much. God can't stand sin either! But no matter how much God hates sin, He loves sinners even more. That is why Jesus came to save sinners and put an end to sin.

Luke records a parable that echoes the situation with Levi well (Luke 18:9–14), "Two men went up into the temple to pray, one a Pharisee and the other a tax collector. The Pharisee stood and was praying this to himself: 'God, I thank You that I am not like other people: swindlers, unjust, adulterers, or even like this tax collector. I fast twice a week; I pay tithes of all that I get' " (verses 10–12). What a record! And probably it was true; he was a great, solid person. At least he felt like one.

There was another person in the temple, however, who had also come to pray; a tax collector. His prayer contrasts strikingly with the other, "But the tax collector, standing some distance away, was even unwilling to lift up his eyes to heaven, but was beating his breast, saying, 'God, be merciful to me, [the] sinner!' " (verse 13; the Greek text has a definite article). This man did not have a list of good deeds to be thankful for. In fact, all he had was his great need, and that's what he brought to God in his prayer. He had come with nothing, but he went home *justified*!

Changed person, unchanged prayer!

What do you suppose would happen to the "justified" tax collector? Doesn't the grace of God transform people? It sure does! So, I imagine that after some time this justified tax collector is no longer a robber or evildoer; he tithes and fasts, and so on. But here is my question, will his prayer ever change and start sounding like the thanks-giving Pharisee? "I thank You Lord that I am not like other people, or like I was, I am so much better now . . ." Well, I certainly hope not. Because the day his prayer changes, he won't be going home justified before God. No matter how much the grace of God transforms us, the prayer of the one justified

Radical Discipleship

by faith remains the same, "God, be merciful to me, *the* sinner."

In this world there is only one Person who will accept you unconditionally. I discovered that later in my life. Having experienced rejection in many forms—because of my own ineptness, or even my own sin—there was always One who accepted me unconditionally. It took me a while to discover and learn the truth of which Paul wrote to the believers in Rome, "For I am convinced that neither death, nor life, nor angels, nor principalities, nor things present, nor things to come, nor powers, nor height, nor depth, nor any other created thing, will be able to separate us from the love of God, which is in Christ Jesus our Lord" (Romans 8:38, 39). Nothing can separate me from God's love, not the rejection I experience from others, not even when I reject and despise myself because of my flaws. You don't have to come to Him with a great résumé. All you need to bring is your great need and you will experience His extraordinary acceptance!

INDIVIDUAL OR SMALL GROUP STUDY QUESTIONS

1. Why do you think Jesus called Levi Matthew to be His disciple?
2. Many unbelievers see Christians as judgmental and critical. What can we do to make the good news of Jesus' extraordinary acceptance real for all?
3. In the Luke 18 parable, why did the tax collector go home "justified" before God?
4. Why was the Pharisee not made right with God? (See Luke 18:9.)
5. Have you experienced the extraordinary acceptance of Jesus?

Chapter 8

EXTRA-Ordinary Calling

I was on the pastoral staff of a large congregation for about twelve years. It had been a fairly comfortable experience. But deep down I knew that my growth in ministry had ground to a halt. I had sensed for a while that God wanted me to move on in order to trust again, to grow again. So when a call came from a smaller congregation, I did not doubt that it was God calling me. However, almost immediately my pragmatism kicked into high gear and spun a ton of questions. *Don't you see that this is a totally different congregation that has had many problems in the past? Are you really prepared to cope with the complexities of ministry there? There have been serious relational issues; do you have the personality and skills to deal with those? God, do You really want me to go there? Are You sure?* Even a well-meaning friend mused, "Why don't you just stay put? You have a good ministry position; things are going well. Why complicate or possibly ruin the stability you enjoy? That congregation is a mess! It's too big of a challenge for you!" And he made a lot of sense—I was not really equipped for that kind of situation! I might end up failing! And then what? The internal struggle, my fear, my heart resistance was overwhelming—and logical! The facts simply did not add up!

And yet, at the same time I felt the beckoning of God, a strange allure to venture into the unknown, to take the leap of faith and to really believe that God does not call the equipped but equips the called. I knew that this was a God-sized challenge, and that it was only God who had resources to deal with it. I did respond to that call. What followed were some of the most difficult times in my life, but also some of the most rewarding and exhilarating times, as I experienced God's extraordinary hand in my life and the life of this congregation and witnessed His miracles as never before.

Ordinary people, EXTRA-ordinary calling!

Philip is a rather unassuming and ordinary disciple. In the listings of

Radical Discipleship

the apostles he is consistently found in the fifth place, in the second circle of disciples. There seems to be nothing spectacular about him. Apart from the lists, he only appears in the Gospel of John in a few brief narratives which shed some light on him. Philip has a Greek name, *Philippos*, and he comes from the small seashore village of Bethsaida (John 12:21).

Philip's character unfolds in the Gospel stories as a man who pays meticulous attention to particulars, a person who always notices the smallest details and worries about them a lot. He seems to be a very pragmatic person who always needs to be in charge of circumstances to make sure everything is under control. In that way Philip is very much like me—I worry a lot, I worry about details, I worry about the results or, rather, the lack of them. I worry about a possible turn of events that may result in things getting out of control, out of *my* control, that is. My mind seems to be programed to think primarily about the practical side and to analyze every situation to death, just like Philip.

Philip is among the first ones to receive the call of Jesus. "The next day He purposed to go into Galilee, and He found Philip. And Jesus said to him, 'Follow Me.' " (John 1:43). Jesus invites Philip to follow Him. And Philip does. He is an ordinary, unassuming small-town guy, with no great wealth, no schooling, and no special skills, and yet Jesus calls him to become His follower. Jesus calls all sorts of people including ordinary people like you and me. Jesus does not look on the outside as we do. He does not look at our accomplishments or how high the social status we have achieved. All He needs is our willingness to surrender our hearts to Him and to follow Him wherever He may lead.

Philip has a missionary gene in him—once he discovered Jesus, he wanted to share the good news. He finds Nathaniel and excitedly (with great detail) tells him about Jesus, "We have found Him of whom Moses in the Law and also the Prophets wrote—Jesus of Nazareth, the son of Joseph" (verse 45). Come on, Philip! Isn't this is a bit too much information and too fast? But if Philip made a mistake in his first missionary endeavor, his comeback to Nathaniel's objection is astute and stems from his pragmatism. "Come and see!" (verse 46). You don't really need a detailed theological treatise or a lengthy explanation, just come and experience Him for yourself.

Isn't that wonderful? What an extraordinary call! And what a powerful response! Way to go, Philip! Isn't he a real spiritual hero? Obviously not.

EXTRA-Ordinary Calling

Receiving and responding to Jesus' call does not make Philip an instant spiritual superman nor did it automatically free him from his flaws and shortcomings. Far from that, he is still weak and flawed, he is still Philip, trying to use logic to manage and analyze his way out of difficult situations. Strangely, this gives me hope, especially when I find myself embroiled again and again in those old patterns of thinking.

GIVE ME THE CALCULATOR, PLEASE!

Philip's flawed, ordinary personality is highlighted in the story about the feeding of a great multitude. Jesus is on a mountainside with His disciples, and "a great crowd" follows Him (John 6:2, 3, NIV). It is late in the day, and everybody is tired and hungry and likely becoming a bit grumpy and rowdy. There might be a conflict brewing, so Philip's logical and analytical mind has probably been going in high gear for a while already, reviewing their resources, or rather the lack of them, and going through various possible scenarios. But Jesus wants Philip to get out of his stagnation and to start looking at the reality from God's perspective. He wants him to realize that he has to trust in and depend on God in all of his challenges.

So Jesus turns to him in order to give him a push, to help him get out of his ordinariness, and "said to Philip, 'Where are we to buy bread, so that these may eat?'" (verse 5). John adds that Jesus has asked him this "to test him" while the real plan is already in place (verse 6). By seemingly leading Philip on, Jesus is actually encouraging him to get out of his box and think big. Philip, however, misses the cue and pulls out his calculator, so to speak, and offers an analysis of the situation purely from the human perspective, "Two hundred denarii worth of bread is not sufficient for them, for everyone to receive a little" (verse 7). Is he right? Of course Philip was right—mathematically, that is! His calculations were spot on; that's how much money was needed. However, he was dead wrong about the reality that Jesus was about to reveal. Because being called to be a disciple of Jesus is being called to behold the *extraordinary*, that which is way above our heads! Philip, why don't you use your own medicine that you offered to Nathanael, "just come and see"? Instead of calculating what you can and what you cannot do, why don't you just surrender the situation to Jesus? Why don't you allow Him to deal with this God-sized problem? Let go of control! No matter how big a supply of resources you may have, it will

Radical Discipleship

never be enough to solve your problems. And remember, Jesus already *has a plan*! He's just waiting to get you on board.

EXTRA-*ORDINARY* EXPERIENCE

And what a miracle it was! Jesus was able to use the ridiculously minuscule amount of food, which a little boy had gladly offered, to miraculously feed the multitude! The leftovers alone by far surpassed the amount of the original resources (verses 10–13). This was Jesus' plan from the beginning, and it still is.

Next time, when God calls you to another challenge, why not try something new—instead of counting your resources and appraising your skills, why not try to focus on Him and trust in His plan? I want to do that! Despite my natural propensity to analyze and count, I want to approach every challenge with the understanding that the outcome is not in my hands but in God's! I know He has a plan. Even though I am aware of my human flaws, I am so privileged to have received the extraordinary call of God, and so have you! Trust in His grace and remember He has a plan. Every situation can be a miracle waiting to happen! Come and see!

INDIVIDUAL OR SMALL GROUP STUDY QUESTIONS

1. How does Jesus treat Philip, a pragmatic disciple like many of us?
2. Why is it important to understand that Jesus' disciples were called by an extraordinary Master? How would that understanding be pivotal for them later on?
3. How does this understanding apply to our salvation and daily lives?
4. What impresses you the most about Jesus' treatment of Philip?
5. Don't we walk by faith and *not* by sight? (See 2 Corinthians 5:7.) How does this relate to "Come and see"?

Chapter 9

EXTRA-Ordinary Compassion

A recently married couple moved into their first home. The wife was very happy and thanked her husband profusely for his efforts to find such a wonderful place. When the work of arranging the furniture was done, exhausted but happy, they retired to bed. Oh, how wonderful it was to relax and rest in their own home!

In the middle of the night, however, the husband was suddenly awoken, "Honey," his wife whispered, "I heard a noise! What if there's a burglar downstairs?" The husband found his baseball bat and went downstairs to investigate. Having found nothing, he came back to bed. The following morning the wife was apologetic and said, "I am sure I heard a noise, but it must have been a dream. I will be more careful next time." Nevertheless, almost the same thing happened the following night too.

"Honey, wake up, I heard a noise downstairs!"

"Darling, don't you remember last night? You must have had another dream!"

"Please, please go and check. What if it is a real burglar this time?"

Regretfully, this turned out to be an almost nightly routine. The all-powerful "what if" seemed to always get the upper hand.

Years later, when they both were retired but still enjoyed the same house, the husband was awakened in the middle of the night by a whisper, "I heard a noise. What if . . ." Half asleep and without saying a word, he grabbed the bat and went downstairs for his nightly rounds. And lo and behold, this time there really was a burglar, just a teenage kid.

The burglar was obviously a novice and was frightened stiff. "I am so sorry, sir! Please, please, forgive me! I beg you not to call the police! I will leave and never come back again!" he pleaded.

But the husband asserted his authority, "No, I can't allow you to leave like that! You have to come upstairs and meet my wife. She has been waiting for you for forty years!"

Don't we all have a little strain of what-ifs in us—expecting the worst

Radical Discipleship

to happen? What if I fail? What if I lose my money? What if I lose my job? What if I get cancer? We spend so much time worrying about things that may or may not happen that we don't have any energy left to move forward.

THE WORRYWART DISCIPLE

Thomas is exactly such a pessimist who constantly worries and keeps asking, "What if?" The proverbial pessimistic Thomas! He always sees the glass half empty and expects the worst possible outcome! In the synoptic Gospels (Matthew, Mark, and Luke) he is mentioned only in the listings of the disciples, while John provides three accounts about him, giving us a better insight into the heart of this man.

We first meet Thomas at the time when the hatred of the temple authorities toward Jesus has reached such depth that they have decided to seek His life. Thomas takes part in the conversation when Jesus has just received the news of the critical illness of his friend Lazarus (John 11:1–15). Jesus wants to go with his disciples to see Lazarus, but they warn him of the danger, "Rabbi, the Jews were just now seeking to stone You, and are You going there again?" (verse 8). Jesus is unshaken but strangely (for them and for us) waits for two more days before embarking on the journey to Bethany. He also informs them of the reason for the delay, "So that you may believe" (verse 15). Isn't that something? A delay of an urgent matter in my life might be beneficial to my faith!

And here we get a glimpse of Thomas as an extreme pessimist. During the discussion of the proposed journey he is all about gloom and doom. He tells the frightened disciples, "Let us also go, so that we may die with Him" (verse 16). Even though he displays remarkable courage and loyalty, his negativity and pessimism obscure these noble traits. It sounds as though he's saying, "Oh well, we are going to die anyway, might as well go with Him."

When you know God is calling you, but find the circumstances complicated, and perhaps even dangerous, can you believe that God can succeed? *Lord, I want to follow You, but what if I fail? I am really not equipped for this challenge; it looks like it simply cannot be done!* How do you deal with a challenge like that? The truth is that the real challenge is not in the adverse circumstances we are facing; it is in the lack of faith and trust! Do you believe that God is with you and, even more important, that for God nothing is impossible?

EXTRA-Ordinary Compassion

DOES ANYONE HAVE A MAP?

The next time we meet Thomas is when Jesus is having an intimate conversation with His discouraged followers. He makes the famous promise of His second return. "Do not let your heart be troubled; believe in God, believe also in Me. . . . I go to prepare a place for you. . . . I will come again and receive you to Myself" (John 14:1–3). This is wonderful news! Even though Jesus is going to leave His disciples, He will come back again to take them home to spend eternity with Him. However Thomas is not convinced. Once again he sees the glass half empty. Hold on, Jesus! It's not so clear! How can we know for sure? What if someone gets lost on the way? He exclaims, "Lord, we don't know where You are going, how do we know the way?" (verse 5). Oh Thomas, why can't you just trust Jesus? You don't have to figure everything out because God has all the answers.

We meet Thomas again, right after the Resurrection, when he dismisses the other disciples' reports that Jesus has risen from the dead. He absolutely refuses to believe until he has some physical evidence for the Resurrection. You can't just believe what others say! What if it's not true? In order to believe he has to see and touch, "Unless I see in His hands the imprint of the nails, and put my finger into the place of the nails, and put my hand into His side, I will not believe" (John 20:25). Thomas sounds very much like a skeptic today, "I will never believe the reality you are talking about unless I have some empirical evidence to back it up. I need more than just faith, I need proof! I cannot believe unless I see and touch!" But Jesus understands Thomas, and how his lack of faith and his what-if attitude to life is affecting him. Jesus does not condemn him. Instead He shows him His extraordinary compassion! When Jesus appears to the disciples again a week later and Thomas is with them (verse 26), He goes straight to the heart of the matter. He does not ignore Thomas' struggles. Amazingly He is willing to meet his conditions. "Reach here with your finger, and see My hands; and reach here your hand and put it into My side; and do not be unbelieving, but believing" (verse 27).

Thomas is stunned by the compassion of Jesus! All of a sudden the glass does not seem so empty anymore. Somehow his what-ifs have vanished! He has given up his need for evidence, proofs, and tests. Jesus has reignited his fledgling faith into a raging fire! And a most beautiful and powerful confession spontaneously escapes his lips, "My Lord and my God!" (verse 28). This

Radical Discipleship

is a genuine leap of faith, a leap from evidence-based existence in the what-if world to a miracle in God's reality, where all things are possible. And this is the *only* time someone in the Gospels calls Jesus "God"—not only "Son of God," which was a royal title for many rulers—but actually God! My God! Isn't it amazing what Jesus' extraordinary compassion creates in our souls?

BLESSED ARE YOU!

Later Jesus said, "Because you have seen Me, have you believed? Blessed are *they* who did not see, and yet believed" (verse 29; emphasis added). *They* include everyone, even you and me, as we eventually believe in Jesus without actually seeing Him. And we are blessed!

Do you find yourself awakened at night by your own what-ifs? Does the glass seem half empty whenever life gets tough? Do you demand evidence before you take a leap of faith? You are in good company. Remember Thomas. Through His extraordinary compassion Jesus turned Thomas's life upside down and inside out! He is active in your life too. The question is—will you allow Him to give you peace through His extraordinary compassion so that He can take away all of your what-ifs and doubts? He died for our sins, rose to life, and has guaranteed our salvation. We can stop expecting the worst and start expecting the best because He is our Lord and our God! And our whole life (present and eternal) is in *His hands*; and believe me, His are more than *capable hands*!

INDIVIDUAL OR SMALL GROUP STUDY QUESTIONS

1. Why do you think Jesus chose Thomas even though he was a worrywart?
2. Many times in the Scriptures we find the exhortation "Do not fear/worry." What does this say about humankind? When did this start? (Read Genesis 3:8, 9.)
3. What is the significance of the confession "My Lord and my God"?
4. Thomas seems to have been a loyal, courageous, and pessimistic disciple. How is that combination possible? Do you identify with any of these characteristics?
5. Read John 14:1–3. Write or talk about what these words of Jesus mean for you today.

Chapter 10

EXTRA-Ordinary Worth

If you Google *self-worth*, you will get pages and pages of stuff on all imaginable aspects of the subject: tests to measure your self-worth, articles on the psychology of self-worth, tips on how to build self-worth, and so on. Self-worth is a big deal and rightly so! Many of us experience a lack of it, which profoundly affects our lives.

Once I met a church member who was struggling with this issue in terms of his religious experience. "Why should I be constantly reminded that I am a sinner, unworthy of God's favor? That really erodes my self-worth! And I need every bit of my self-worth in order to function and even survive in this dog-eat-dog world. How is Christianity contributing to my self-worth? Or is it?"

Well, that is a *very* good question! First of all, the pecking order and the Wild West mentality that dominate our society make it rather difficult to maintain a healthy self-worth. It is especially true for those of us who are somewhat less socially endowed and, perhaps, feel a little bit like underdogs. But the important question is: Does my Christian experience help me build self-worth or does it erode it?

I have struggled with low self-worth for a very long time. My early, traumatic experiences of growing up in a society hostile to God, where those who believed in God were considered somewhat less than normal, had affected my personality. And I have always found it difficult to fit in and feel like I belong. Early on, my religion did not help either as I was always focusing on my flaws and my failed efforts to be good enough. Only later in life did I make the radical discovery of my worth in Jesus Christ. I experienced the paradox that every self-hating and socially inept sinner is bound to see when presented with the real Jesus! You are loved and valued and accepted not because you are good enough, but simply because you are a child of God, created in His image.

Radical Discipleship

JAMES WHO?

We can surmise pretty safely that three of the disciples of Jesus—James (not John's brother), Judas (not the betrayer), and Simon (not Peter)—likely had some issues with self-worth. Hierarchically they are always mentioned in the bottom group of four, along with Judas, the one who would betray Jesus. There is almost nothing mentioned about them in the Gospels besides their names. Yet, they reach out to us from obscurity with a definite message of encouragement—God sees an extraordinary value in you.

James, the son of Alphaeus, unlike his namesake—is almost invisible in the Gospels. His name (Greek *Iakóbos*) is of Hebrew origin; it was the name of the patriarch Jacob and carries the distinct connotation of dishonesty. An interesting and significant detail that we do know about James is his nickname, *the Less* or *the Younger* (Mark 15:40). The Greek word used here is *mikros,* which has found its way into the English language in such words as *microscope* and *microbe.* He likely got his nickname from his peers who merely wanted to make a distinction between the two namesakes. Whatever the reason for the nickname, it must have affected the already-fragile self-image of James. Remember, according to the lists of the disciples, he was at the very bottom of the apostolic pecking order. Imagine your name is Rick but there's someone else in your group with the same name, and therefore everyone calls you Ricky because you are younger, shorter, or simply a lot less important. How would you feel about it?

There are so many people in this world, including myself, who do not think of themselves too highly and therefore constantly struggle. There are plenty of examples in the Bible too. Think of people such as Paul, Gideon, or Moses and countless others. The common denominator among these people is that at one point or another they all felt worthless and thought that God could not possibly use them because of who they were or what they had done. But, paradoxically, God used these exact people powerfully to accomplish His purposes.

Jesus said, "The kingdom of heaven is like a mustard seed, . . . and this is smaller [*mikros*] than all other seeds, but when it is full grown, it is larger [*meizon*, a Greek comparative of *megas*] than the garden plants" (Matthew 13:31, 32). In God's kingdom the conventional human values are reversed. God specifically uses those who feel insignificant, weak, and unimportant, those who do not consider themselves strong enough or wise enough to be self-reliant and therefore have to trust in God. In Luke 9:46–48 an argument arises among the disciples as to who is the greatest. Just like us today, they crave greatness, importance, and worth. Jesus brings a little child into their midst and says, "For the one who is least [*mikros*] among all of you, this is the one who is great [*megas*]." I can imagine James, the *mikros*, excitedly waving his hands. "Finally someone talks about us *mikros*! I do have a place in the kingdom of heaven after all!"

NOT THAT ONE!

Judas is introduced as the son of James (Luke 6:16). Judas is the Greek version of the Hebrew name Judah, meaning "praise." It was a very popular name among the Jews in first-century Palestine because it was derived from the tribe of Judah (see Genesis 29:35). Mark and Matthew use the name Thaddeus (Mark 3:18).

John, however, simply calls him Judas—but with an important disclaimer—*not Iscariot* (John 14:22). It is not hard to imagine why the disclaimer is used. Judas Iscariot, his namesake, was notorious with his treacherous treason. Poor Judas Thaddeus probably felt as if he were constantly living in the dark shadow of Iscariot. Whenever he was introduced to people, everybody assumed this was Iscariot. And who would want to associate with the notorious traitor? Judas had to constantly deal with mistaken identity and go through life having to defend his good name! It was like living with a big sign on one's forehead: I am Judas, but NOT THAT ONE!

Judas appears briefly in John's Gospel. The disciples are engaged in a conversation with Jesus about His death and subsequent departure to heaven. The disciples find it very hard to understand the impending reality and therefore frequently interrupt Jesus with genuine questions. There's Peter, then Thomas, and Philip, all asking questions. Jesus answers patiently and in detail. Finally, Judas finds a little break in the conversation to present his question, "Lord, what then has happened that You are going to disclose Yourself to us and not to the world?" (verse 22). In other words, "Jesus, why don't You reveal Yourself to the world in a more spectacular way? The Old Testament is filled with magnificent and glorious scenes of the coming of the Messiah! Why isn't Your kingdom more pronounced?" Judas means well, and he wants to help Jesus understand the big picture, to show the people a bigger and more spectacular Christianity, to prove to the world that this is a very impressive and respectable religion! The man that always had to prove to the world who he *really* was, now wants Jesus to do the same. Why allow for a mistaken identity when You can really *show* who You *really* are?

Judas, however, does not realize that no one is able to think *bigger* than Jesus. So He has to put things in perspective for Judas and his companions. The defining, and most crucial, thing for Jesus is not external pomp and spectacle but *love* that works on the inside. He says, "If anyone loves Me, he will keep My word; and My Father will love him, and We will come to him and make Our abode with him" (verse 23). The important thing is not a big religious parade, an external show of power to impress the world, but a deep, quiet understanding of God's extraordinary grace that affects the heart and works its way out into the world and eventually permeates it.

A PASSIONATE GOD

Simon (not Peter) also has a nickname—Zealot. We can only guess what kind of zealot Simon was. Maybe he was a member of the outlawed resistance movement called Zealots that violently opposed the Roman power. Or perhaps he was simply very passionate by nature. The Bible does not give us any clues about it. However, he does reveal to us something about his personality through his nickname. Passion, rightly directed, is a very desirable characteristic to have. As a matter of fact, we can't do without it. In Revelation 3:15 a derivative of the same Greek word is used in the description of the Laodicean church. It is neither hot (*zestos*) nor cold but lukewarm instead. Being lukewarm is a very serious condition that God will not tolerate. And therefore Jesus offers this church a specific remedy for their lukewarmness.

However, the truth is that we are unable to fabricate real passion. It overflows out of God's grace. Paul was naturally an "extremely zealous" person (Galatians 1:14), yet his zeal being focused on religiosity and tradition was very destructive, not the kind of passion we want. Only when he experienced God's grace did he become exclusively passionate about Jesus and nothing else (1 Corinthians 2:2). The same happens with us. Once we experience God's incredible grace we will not and cannot remain the same. And the truth is that it is not just that God wants *us* to be passionate about Him; *He Himself* has been revealed to us as a very passionate God. In the second commandment (Exodus 20:5) God calls Himself a "jealous God." The Hebrew word for jealous reminds us of Simon the Zealot. God is passionate about you!

God's grace has no bounds! Jesus came to die for us and to redeem us, to give us the undeserved, free gift of salvation. Through His sacrifice He carried out the ancient covenantal promise—God will be our God and we will be His people. And when we receive the extraordinary grace of God, He ignites in us an uncontainable passion, which will spill into every aspect of our lives. We will find our worth, identity, and purpose at the feet of Jesus. And that, my friend, is a life worth living!

INDIVIDUAL OR SMALL GROUP STUDY QUESTIONS

1. What is *real* worth and why is it found only at the foot of the cross?
2. Explain the kingdom's principle of "the first shall be last and the last shall be first."
3. How does God *show* Himself to the world? Why doesn't He use more "forceful" and "visibly convincing" ways to earn people's allegiance?
4. Does God want us to be passionate? How does He redirect our zeal?
5. How does God's extraordinary grace produce a sense of extraordinary worth in us, in light of His salvific act on our behalf?

Chapter 11

EXTRA-Ordinary Perseverance

In his book *The Gospel According to Judas*, Ray S. Anderson shares an experience, "I saw it in the men's restroom in a restaurant in San Francisco, printed in block letters with a blue felt tip pen across the top of the mirror: JUDAS, COME HOME—ALL IS FORGIVEN!" These words made me think, could it really be possible that Judas could be forgiven? How about the worst of the worst among us, such as Hitler, Stalin, or modern-day terrorists? Is there a point of no return in human life, spiritually speaking? If I insist on running away from God and persevere in shutting God out of my life, is there a point at which God says, "That's it! I've had it with you!"? I feel that way whenever I read in the news of yet another barbaric murder of innocent victims! But how about God? Does God ever get fed up with any of us?

Judas may very well be the most detested man in history, as his name has become a synonym for utmost betrayal. In the *Divine Comedy*, Dante Alighieri depicts Judas being punished in the worst possible part of hell, designed specifically for those traitors who have betrayed their benefactors.

A THIEF? WHAT WAS JESUS THINKING?

The Gospels mention Judas often but with a notation about his betrayal, such as, "Judas Iscariot, one of His disciples, who was intending to betray Him" (John 12:4). Judas is the only one among the disciples who was given a specific function. He was the treasurer, responsible for managing their funds (John 13:29). In business, when an important vacancy is to be filled, candidates submit their résumés and every aspect of their lives and characters are scrutinized, and then the very best is selected to hold the position. We know that on Judas's résumé Jesus could foresee at least two major flaws, two humongous issues that would surely disqualify any candidate today.

First of all, Judas was a dishonest man. He wasn't just telling a little white lie here and there; he was actually a big-time embezzler. John reveals this dark truth in the story of a special meal in Bethany. Jesus and His disciples are invited for dinner, and Lazarus, whom Jesus has just raised from the dead, is there as well. Mary uses the occasion to do something unexpected—breaking all conventions. She sneaks into the room filled with male guests and secretly anoints Jesus' feet, hoping that nobody will notice. But she overlooks one thing—the oil she uses. The nard oil has an extremely strong scent and fills the house with its sweet fragrance. Now everyone knows what Mary has done. Judas, the financier, takes the floor and declares, "Why was this perfume not sold for three hundred denarii and given to poor people?" Great idea, Judas! You really care for the poor, don't you? However, John adds a revealing and damaging piece of information to Judas's résumé. He was not concerned about the poor at all but spoke because "he was a thief, and as he had the money box, he used to pilfer what was put into it" (John 12:5, 6). That's no small matter! One could go to jail for embezzlement. Yet Jesus took Judas as His treasurer!

Second, the Bible is clear that Jesus knew that Judas would betray Him. Why in the world would Jesus take Judas for a disciple, let alone the treasurer? In the Latvian language there are many great and funny idioms that feature all kinds of animals. One such idiom comes to mind to fittingly describe the situation with Judas as the group's treasurer—"to hire a goat for a gardener." The implication is that a goat, put in charge of a garden, would graze all the greenery and eventually destroy it. Why would Jesus choose a person who would become so destructive? Why couldn't He choose someone else? We know that He did not do it for lack of knowledge about what kind of person Judas was, and not for the lack of qualified people available for the position either. He must have done it for another reason.

A thief and a traitor!

Really! What was Jesus thinking? Ironically, after his piously hypocritical speech about the poor, Judas went straight to the chief priests and sold Jesus to them for thirty pieces of silver (Matthew 26:14–16). Yet Jesus, knowing all of his hypocrisy, still called him to discipleship, accepted, and welcomed him. He did it because He loved Judas and wanted to win his heart. He wanted to expose Judas to His grace and give him every chance to accept it. He was pursuing Judas's heart with an extraordinary perseverance.

Would I take Judas for *my* treasurer? Think about the implications! Actually there is a Judas in every one of us, just waiting for an opportunity to

Radical Discipleship

come out, to have our own Judas moment. And the question is—would I take *myself* for a treasurer? Knowing what I know about myself, would I take myself for a disciple? Jesus knows us better than we do; He knows everything about us—even the darkest secrets hidden within. Yet He loves us. His love does not depend on our goodness; He just loves us. And He will keep pursuing our hearts to the very end. As long as there is time, He will never give up.

John, in chapter 13, provides a good insight into that extraordinary perseverance with which Jesus pursued Judas, His traitor. Jesus and His disciples are in a private room one last time, breaking bread together. The setting is right before His death on the cross which will be the result of Judas's treachery. Yet, Jesus does not give up on Judas. We can clearly see how He is bending over backward to demonstrate to Judas His extraordinary love. Even though there are at least six mentions in this chapter about the impending betrayal, the narrative is bracketed (an *inclusio*—narrative bookends) with an assurance of Jesus' love. John introduces the narrative with, "Having loved His own who were in the world, He loved them to the end" (verse 1). John is making sure the reader understands that Jesus had lived a life of pure love from the beginning to the end, but now, as He was nearing His death, there was yet one more demonstration of His love left to be shown to the disciples, and most of all to Judas. Then John concludes the chapter with Jesus' exhortation to love, "Love one another, even as I have loved you" (verse 34). Thus, John has set the stage to show the reader how Jesus treats His traitor.

HEAVENLY PERSEVERANCE

Jesus is trying to win Judas back through four specific acts of love. First of all, there are no slaves to wash their feet, which is an expected service. Jesus takes on the role of a slave, the role no one else is willing to take, and washes the disciples' feet—including the dirty feet of Judas.

Second, from the context of the narrative, we can reasonably conclude that Judas is seated next to Jesus in the second most honorable place. As the customs of the time suggest, Jesus is probably seated in the place of the host, at the bottom of the U-shaped table, and John is occupying a seat next to Him (verses 23, 25). Judas is sitting on the other side since Jesus could give him bread (verse 26) and could speak to him privately

(Matthew 26:25). The best seat for the traitor! Would you have done so?

Third, when John makes a private request to Jesus to point out the traitor, He responds with an action that remains private, in terms of delivering the answer, yet is very public in honoring Judas. He hands Judas a piece of bread which, in that culture, would be understood as a mark of great honor (John 13:26). That way, Jesus makes a public spectacle honoring His traitor. Would you do that? Would I do that? Just think about the one person in your life who has wronged you the most—would you honor such a person for everyone to see?

And, finally, Jesus never yields to the pressure to identify the traitor publicly. Instead, all through the evening Jesus is sending Judas signals of His love and assurances of His grace and proofs of His utmost respect. John is making sure we understand that Jesus never gives up on trying to win Judas back, to restore the relationship with him. He keeps trying to the very last, to the very end, all the way to the cross. Paul puts it succinctly, "While we were yet sinners, Christ died for us" (Romans 5:8).

IS THERE FORGIVENESS FOR ME?

Unfortunately, Judas totally misses all the signals of love from Jesus, but, instead, "went out immediately; and it was night" (John 13:30). This statement is highly symbolic because there is more night in the heart of Judas than the darkness outside. He proceeds to carry out his treacherous deed. Matthew describes the aftermath of his betrayal. "When Judas, who had betrayed Him, saw that He had been condemned, he felt remorse and returned the thirty pieces of silver to the chief priests and the elders, saying, 'I have sinned by betraying innocent blood' " (Matthew 27:3, 4). So Judas felt remorse! Interestingly, Matthew juxtaposes this with the fact that during the same night Peter denies Jesus, thus, also betraying and sinning against Him (Matthew 26:69–75). And having realized what he had done, Peter "wept bitterly" (verse 75). So Peter felt remorse as well! Both men felt remorse; however, there was a huge difference between the two and where each of them ended up. The Greek word used in Matthew 27:3 regarding Judas is *metamelētheis,* which means "regret" or "changing ones' mind." Judas regretted the fact that his plan had backfired and went out and hanged himself. Peter, on the other hand, repented and was transformed into a powerful preacher of the gospel. The biggest problem for Judas was his rejection of the countless demonstrations of the love and grace of Jesus. The only difference between the two was that Peter chose to believe that God's grace was sufficient and Jesus' blood was enough to cover his sin, while Judas did not. We don't claim to know the eternal fate of any soul, but it is important to ask this question: what would have happened if, instead of killing himself, Judas would have gone to the cross and in true repentance accepted the forgiveness of Jesus? Jesus had already made provision for him, because forgiveness precedes repentance and draws the sinner to ask for what is already offered freely; that's exactly why Jesus was on the cross. But, unfortunately, as far as we know, Judas never accepted that love and that forgiveness.

JUDAS, COME HOME—ALL IS FORGIVEN!

Judas has something to tell each one of us today. The truth is that all of the disciples betrayed Jesus. In fact, all of us find ourselves in the same boat. What are we going to do with Jesus' extraordinary perseverance, His love and grace that He constantly sends our way? Are we going to take matters in our own hands, like Judas? Or, like Peter, are we going to listen to heaven's whisper telling all the Judases of the world, "Come home, Judas! Jesus loves you, all's forgiven!"? The choice is yours and mine.

INDIVIDUAL OR SMALL GROUP STUDY QUESTIONS

1. What happens when a bitter heart is left unchecked?
2. Does God want to save everyone?
3. Why did Jesus allow Judas to handle the money bag?
4. Is there enough provision at the Cross for any and all sins? (Read Hebrews 10:11–14.)
5. Even though both betrayed Jesus, Peter and Judas ended up in very different places. One preached sermons used by God to convert thousands. The other hanged himself. What was the main difference between the two?

Chapter 12

EXTRA-Ordinary Encounter

We are almost at the end of our journey with the close friends of Jesus. We discovered that the followers whom Jesus chose were no spiritual superheroes in any shape or form. They were ordinary and flawed people, just like you and me, who constantly struggled and failed and never quite measured up to what they were supposed to be. They were not impressive CEOs and business executives (by today's standards), instead they were a messy band of ragtags. Discipleship is messy, just as life itself is messy. But we have also discovered that when we encounter the real Jesus and decide to follow Him, we will live the rest of our lives in wonder and awe about His grace and love. His followers are ordinary people who have accepted God's extraordinary grace and, thus, are living in a continuous miracle.

But there is still one more disciple who, though not one of the twelve, yet, was called by Jesus Himself to be His apostle. Let's take a look at this other disciple, Paul, or Saul, as he was known prior to his calling. He was the one who received a special call from Jesus not only to follow Him but to be the apostle for the Gentiles, beyond the borders of Israel (Galatians 1:1; Acts 9:15).

THE PASSIONATE SAUL OF TARSUS

Saul was born in Tarsus, southeast Asia Minor (part of today's Turkey). His parents had a Jewish background yet were Roman citizens. Even though Judea was within the Roman Empire, Jews were not automatically Roman citizens. Citizenship outside Italy was conferred only as an honor for special contributions to the empire (or when certain slaves bought their emancipation and became free men). Thus, it is likely that Saul's parents were important people with considerable means. Saul trained under the prominent rabbi, Gamaliel, and received the best possible education of the time (Acts 22:3). As was the custom, he also learned a practical trade (tent making) to fall back on in case of an emergency.

Radical Discipleship

Paul was a man of action, a very passionate person. When he saw a threat to Judaism, he would always spring to action with resolve in order to eliminate it. Christianity became such a threat, so he began deadly attacks on Christians with ferocious passion. While addressing a crowd in Jerusalem, Paul recounts his early life, "[I was] zealous for God just as you all are today. I persecuted this Way to the death, binding and putting both men and women into prisons" (verses 3, 4). That is a very revealing statement! Paul says he was *zealous and passionate for God*! That's great and wonderful, isn't it? Anyone who is passionate for God must be following God's will, right? The point that Paul is making here is extremely important. Religious fervor by and of itself does not guarantee that a person is right with God. It is possible for one to be a religious zealot, passionate about God, and at the same time be terribly wrong and evil—Paul was. He was zealous for God and, at the same time, persecuted the followers of the Way (Christians) to death. Thus, it is possible to be passionate about God, to know about Him from the Bible, and yet not know Him. There is a world of difference between knowing about God and knowing God. Jesus said, "You search the Scriptures because you think that in them you have eternal life; it is these that testify about Me; and you are unwilling to come to Me so that you may have life" (John 5:39, 40). Is it then OK to study the Bible? Is it OK to be passionately religious? Of course it is! It is necessary! But it's not the Bible reading or the religion that gives us life; those things are in service to a much greater Reality: they are to lead us to Jesus Christ! And, therefore, unless we have encountered the Life-Giver Himself, all other things, good as they are, will not help us. In fact, as we have seen in Paul's experience, a religion without God and the Scriptures without Jesus can actually make a person worse and incite a destructive behavior.

GETTING KNOCKED OFF THE HORSE

Paul was zealous and extremely religious as well as destructive. We meet him first in Acts 7 and 8 in the narrative of Stephen's stoning, giving us an indication of where Saul stands in this, "Saul was in hearty agreement with putting him to death" (Acts 8:1). Further on, "still breathing threats and murder against the disciples of the Lord" (Acts 9:1), we see Saul taking another initiative to persecute and eliminate the followers of Jesus. Some of the Christians find refuge from persecution outside the borders of Jerusalem, for example, in Damascus. Saul, having secured permission from the high priest to extradite those refugees back to Jerusalem (verses 1, 2), gets on the road to hunt down the followers of Jesus.

However, this trip becomes an earth-shattering and life-changing experience for Saul as he unexpectedly encounters Jesus on the road to Damascus. "As he was traveling, it happened that he was approaching Damascus, and suddenly a light from heaven flashed around him; and he fell to the ground and heard a voice saying to him, 'Saul, Saul, why are you persecuting Me?' And he said, 'Who are You, Lord?' And He said, 'I am Jesus whom you are persecuting, but get up and enter the city, and it will be told you what you must do' " (verses 3–6). After meeting Jesus, Saul's life is forever changed, even his name changes to Paul. From a vicious and murderous persecutor of Christians he is turned into a passionate and relentless preacher of the gospel of Jesus Christ. He becomes God's chosen instrument to carry the message of hope and salvation to the Gentiles (Acts 9:15). It is nothing short of a miracle! How is it possible to have such a *radical* change, a complete U-turn?

This is an amazing testimony about what happens when a person encounters Jesus Christ. The personality traits that were previously in the service of evil, control, and destruction, in the name of God, are now used by God for the service of good. Saul's passion had been used to pursue religion and to persecute those who did not agree with him. Now, after Paul's extraordinary encounter with Jesus, the same passion lost its destructiveness and found a positive direction for bringing the good news of the gospel to the world. And let me tell you something: God will make sure each one of us gets a "knocked off our horse" kind of experience! He will give each one of us a chance to encounter His extraordinary grace through Jesus! And many of us find the *real Jesus* in such an experience after years of religiosity.

I AM NOT ASHAMED OF THE GOSPEL!

Paul's passion for Christ was an all-consuming, entire-life-permeating, all-else-devaluing force that animated his life and mission. He wrote about it to the believers in Philippi, "But whatever things were gain to me, those things I have counted as loss for the sake of Christ. More than that,

Radical Discipleship

I count all things to be loss in view of the surpassing value of knowing Christ Jesus my Lord, for whom I have suffered the loss of all things, and count them but rubbish so that I may gain Christ, . . . that I may know Him and the power of His resurrection" (Philippians 3:7–10). There we have it—the reversal of values that Jesus introduced! What was profitable in the past now amounts to a complete loss! The most valuable thing now is to know Christ, to have Him in our lives, to live in His presence, and to accept His righteousness as a gift. Nothing, absolutely nothing, in this world equals having Christ in our lives and finding ourselves at peace with God through Him. Paul can't even find words to express his passion, so he resorts to some "French," some unconventional language. The word translated in English as "rubbish" (verse 8) is *skubalon* in Greek, meaning "dung." That's a very strong word to use in the Bible, isn't it? Sometimes Bible translators try to soften the impact of words and sanitize the language to make it more appropriate. But Paul had a passion for Christ that needed to be expressed! And God would rather have us real than proper. The good news of righteousness by faith through Christ is now Paul's ultimate goal and pursuit. Nothing, absolutely nothing, in this world compares with that one goal—knowing Christ crucified on our behalf. Writing to believers in Corinth, he wrote, "For I determined to know nothing among you except Jesus Christ, and Him crucified" (1 Corinthians 2:2). And in that original, extraordinary encounter with Jesus, Paul found the core purpose of his life. He found what the gospel *really* means because it became his story and he was forever sticking to it! "For I am not ashamed of the gospel, for *it is the power of God for salvation to everyone who believes,* to the Jew first and also to the Greek. For in it the righteousness of God is revealed, from faith to faith, as it is written, 'BUT THE RIGHTEOUS MAN SHALL LIVE BY FAITH' " (Romans 1:16, 17; emphasis added). *Not ashamed*! Totally convinced that *Jesus is the only way* to salvation!

PARADOXICAL DISCIPLESHIP: WHEN I AM WEAK, THEN I AM STRONG!

What is the ultimate passion in my life? What does my heart yearn for the most? What is that one thing that fills the void in my heart? Living

EXTRA-Ordinary Encounter

is *all about Jesus*! Discipleship is not about achievements; it's not about climbing the ladder of virtues. It's not even about getting your act together. The truth is, we will never get our acts together, not to the degree that would earn our salvation. The only *act* that is together and completed and really counts is that of Jesus. And when we have Him in our hearts and our lives, we have the assurance of salvation. Then little by little, as we trust Him more and more, He will be able to transform us and change our hearts and redirect our passions and use us powerfully for good, all for His glory and to enlarge His kingdom. He will be able to use us in spite of our weaknesses and flaws. Just as He used Paul, who said, "For when I am weak, then I am strong" (2 Corinthians 12:10). *Discipleship is not a list of dos and don'ts; it is a life of constant wonder and awe about the grace of God. It is what happens when ordinary people accept His EXTRA-ordinary grace.*

INDIVIDUAL OR SMALL GROUP STUDY QUESTIONS

1. How can a religious Bible student like Paul, with zeal for God, end up working against God's purposes? Is it possible to be an honest follower of God and, in the name of religion, persecute other people?
2. What was the pivotal point in Paul's experience? Why?
3. Why are many people so eager to talk about all the things they are doing for God, as if these things make them appear more zealous and perhaps more deserving of God's salvation?
4. What exactly is the gospel of Jesus Christ that Paul said he was not ashamed of? (Read Romans 1:16, 17.) What does it mean to know nothing "except Jesus Christ and Him crucified"? (See 1 Corinthians 2:2.)
5. Write a definition of a disciple of Jesus: _____

_____

I, _____, want to be a disciple of Jesus and receive His EXTRA-ordinary grace!

For additional FREE resources, videos on demand, daily devotionals, biblical studies, audio books, and much more, please visit our Web site:

www.Jesus101.tv

If you have been blessed by this booklet and would like to help us keep spreading the good news of Jesus Christ through preaching, teaching, and writing, please send your donations to

Jesus 101

Jesus 101 Biblical Institute
P. O. Box 10008
San Bernardino, CA 92423

WATCH the JESUS 101 channel on ROKU!

DOWNLOAD the JESUS 101 app TODAY!